THE EXPERIENCES OF A CARE-GIVER

JOHN KESHI

Fulton Books
Meadville, PA

Published by Fulton Books 2022

To protect the privacy of individuals names
in this book have been changed.

ISBN 978-1-63985-896-5 (paperback)
ISBN 979-8-88505-222-1 (hardcover)
ISBN 978-1-63985-897-2 (digital)

Dedicated to my grandmother.

THE EARLY YEARS

I was born in Asaba, a Nigerian town by the River Niger. It was once a rural community. When we were kids, we woke up at the first crow of the cock and set out for the river with clay pots befitting our sizes, to shower and to fetch water, before setting out for school weekdays. Mr. Udoka was one of my teachers in middle school. He was short and plump, with an oblong head. He rarely smiled. People with the same head shape were reputed to be very smart. He was good in class. He knew his stuff. Mr. Udoka was a true professional. He attended a top-flight teacher's training college and graduated with distinction. He always wore khaki shorts with a white short-sleeved shirt and long white stockings that reached his knees. His solid brown leather shoes were so shiny you could see the reflection of your face in them. It was rumored in school that he spent a considerable amount of time each day at home polishing his shoes. Evidently, his appearance meant a lot to him, and he aspired to be a good role model for his students. Mr. Udoka had an aura of authority about him. His utterances to his students were delivered like facts coming from some kind of imperial figure. They were not to be contradicted. His students had no choice. It was either we followed his instructions or we got in trouble.

The school was a coeducational government school. The buildings were made of solid cement blocks with large doors and windows, and it was fenced. There was a big gate at the front entrance. We were expected to be in school at eight o'clock in the morning. Tardiness was not tolerated. We were punished whenever we arrived late. We received six lashes of a whip on our butt. Some students wore three or four shorts. Another batch of students went as far as stuffing their shorts with rags to lessen the pain from the whips. There was the case of a student who was oblivious to the string jutting out of his shorts. It caught the attention of Mr. Udoka. The student was summoned before him. "Turn around," said Mr. Udoka. The student turned around. "What is that coming out of your shorts?" he asked. The whole class started laughing. We knew what it was, but Mr. Udoka was in the dark. He was later told through the grapevine that some students cushioned their buttocks with rags to lessen the impact of the punishment they received when they arrived late. From then on, he examined the shorts of latecomers to ensure that they were wearing just one pair of shorts. Tardy female students received their lashes on their palms.

Mr. Udoka expected absolute silence while teaching. He was not a happy man when distracted by the noise made by students. Some students exchanged love letters with their girlfriends while in class, which sometimes generated whispers. Mr. Udoka would turn around and face the class. "I don't have eyes at the back of my head, but my hearing is good. Who was whispering, and why?" he would ask. The classroom was as quiet as an abandoned house. "Who was whispering, and why?" he would repeat. "I am not speaking Latin. You boys and girls understand me," he would add. Angry now he would say, "Okay, the whole class is going to be punished if no one is willing to speak up!" The whole class was sometimes punished by making everybody kneel by our desk and raise our hands up. It was up to him to tell us when to stand up and put down our hands. It depended on his mood. It was tough on us when it was a long-term punishment.

Sometimes, Emeka, a tall slim student, would raise his hands and point out the culprits before the whole class was punished. Emeka was a good student, and many of us liked him, although a handful of classmates did not get along with him for his role as a snitch. It seemed the troublemakers had fun by giving Mr. Udoka a hard time. On the other hand, those of us who sided with Emeka felt it was not proper for the entire class to be punished for the foolery of two classmates.

The dislike some of our classmates had for Emeka did not last long, especially when the fruits were ripe on the trees and available. With his slim figure and long arms and legs, Emeka was a good climber. Tall trees were not challenges to him. He mounted them with ease. When fruits like mango, guava, and *udala* were ripe and far up on the trees, Emeka was our man. He was the man of the moment. Sometimes, after school, we followed him to orchards owned by his relatives. With remarkable ease, he climbed up the tall trees and brought us ripe fruits. At other times, he brought the fruits in bags to school and shared it with us during our break.

In middle school, our physical education class was fun. One of the games we played was "There is fire on the mountain." We paired up with our partners and stood in a wide circle. The partners standing behind would run around the circle while Mr. Udoka chanted, "There is fire on the mountain. Run, run, run. There is fire on the mountain. Run, run, run." When he said "the fire is over," we were expected to pair up with our partners. The last partners to pair up lost that particular round of the race. This exercise would go on until it was just two students standing. They were the winners. At other times, we ran sack races. These were full of falls and laughter, but most of us preferred pairing up with partners and running around the circle.

On Saturdays, we went to the farm to help out with the farmwork. At the end of the day, we brought back firewood for our mothers' cook fires. On the way to the farm, we came across hunters who had gone to the forest before dawn to hunt deer. Sometimes they had their kills attached to the carriers on their bicycles.

Farming in Asaba was mostly subsistence. It was largely for family consumption. Very few farmers sold their crops to outsiders. The planting season followed the rainfalls. Before the arrival of the rains, the farmers had to clear vast acres of virgin land. Trees were cut down with axes and machetes. It was left for some time to dry and then set on fire. Smoke from the fires rose high into the sky and attracted large birds that flew in circles while letting out sharp shrieks that created enormous noise. It was as if the birds were complaining about the destruction of nature. It was quite a sound and sight to behold.

Yam was an important crop cultivated by the farmers. A farmer who could feed his family on yams from one planting season to another was considered a successful farmer. When the soil had been moistened by heavy rains, farmers, along with their families, went to their farms with seed yams and farming implements, and the planting season started. Mounds made of earth in straight lines covered vast acres of farmland. Yam seeds were planted in the mounds. A successful harvest demanded much attention. It had to be protected from too much sun and very heavy rains. At appropriate times, the yams were held up with tiny sticks and then later with large sticks or tree branches. Then came the weeding. The weeds around the yam had to be cleared. We accomplished this task with hoes, a long wooden farming implement with a metallic blade. We spent hours weeding, bending our backs, covering many miles of farmland. We took several breaks. At the end of the day, we, the young and inexperienced, amateur farmers, suffered from backaches along with swollen and blistered hands. When I showed my swollen hands to my cousin, a professional farmer, he said, "Farming is necessary, but it is not an easy job. Be serious with your schoolwork, and aim for a better future. We all have to eat, and this is why farming is important." I agreed with him that we all had to eat. It is one thing all of humanity share in common. We all need food.

Cocoyam and cassava were also planted on the farm but were mostly allotted to the farmers' wives. The two crops were less exacting than yam. To plant cassava, the women had to dig small holes in the ground with hoes, then cassava stalks that were already cut were placed halfway into the holes and covered with dirt. Cassava can be left in the ground for years without going bad. This is not the case with yams. Although yam is considered the king of crops in certain communities, when it came to longevity, cassava had an edge over yam.

During moonlight nights, young men went to visit their friends. Kids gathered in front of homes and played. Sometimes we were told folk tales from olden times. Storytelling was a way of connecting with and entertaining family members, friends, and neighbors. It was raised to an art form by our fore-bears. Good storytellers stirred the emotion and feeling of their listeners, held their audience in rapt attention, and kept them asking for more. One of the stories I found interesting and fascinating as a kid was the tale of the "Tortoise and the Birds."

The birds were invited to a feast in the sky. They were very glad about the invitation since there was famine in the land at that time. The birds began preparation for the feast. They went to great lengths to beautify themselves, painted their wings in mul-tiple colors, and worked on their personal manner-isms. They left no stone unturned in their prepara-tion. They wanted to impress their host.

Tortoise the wily one, on seeing the preparation the birds were making, asked what it was all about.

"We are invited to a feast in the sky," replied the birds. Tortoise was affected by the famine in the land as well. He had not eaten a good meal for quite some time. He began planning how to join the birds for the feast in the sky. Tortoise was wingless. He could not fly, yet he asked the birds if he could join them.

"You have no wings, you cannot fly," replied the birds.

"Each of you can lend me a feather with which to make two wings," replied Tortoise.

"You are not a stranger to us. We know your cunning and ungratefulness," replied the birds.

"I am a new man. I have discarded my old habits," said Tortoise. "I have learned not to make trouble until trouble itself troubles me," added Tortoise.

Tortoise was a voluble and sometimes convincing speaker. He won over the birds with his persuasive speech. The birds agreed he was a changed man. They each gave him a feather with which he formed two wings. On the appointed day, Tortoise was the first to arrive at the meeting point from which they would take off. When all the birds were assembled, they set out as a group. The entourage was in a happy mood. They talked animatedly among themselves. Tortoise, with his oratory skill, was chosen as the leader of the group.

"There is an ancient and important tradition associated with a feast such as we have been invited to," said Tortoise as they flew along. "When friends had been invited to an august occasion such as this, they take on new names. Our host would be looking forward to this important custom," he added.

The birds knew nothing of this tradition. On the other hand, they knew that Tortoise was a widely traveled man, he had knowledge of many things, and that he knew the customs of many people. The birds accepted the assertion made by Tortoise as true. They each took on new names. Tortoise was to be known as You All. After a long flight, the entourage arrived at their destination. They were greeted by their host. Tortoise, as the spokesman for the birds, stood and thanked their host for the invitation. He was so eloquent in his speech the host assumed he must be the leader.

After the birds and tortoise had shared some appetizers, the host brought out rich and warm meals fresh from the kitchen. There were many dishes, lots to eat and drink. The host said, "The food is for you all" and left. Tortoise, being the greedy and gluttonous type, reminded the birds that they had taken new names before their arrival and that he was to be known as You All. Tortoise ate the best dishes, and the birds had to eat the leftovers. The birds were not happy at the treatment meted out to them by Tortoise whom they had brought along out of their own kindness. They were aghast and decided to take back the feathers they had earlier lent to Tortoise before going back home.

Tortoise was full. He had eaten enormously but had no way of getting back home. He asked the birds to take a message on his behalf to his wife. The birds were so disgusted by the appalling conduct of Tortoise that all but one bird consented to his request. Tortoise asked the consenting bird to tell his wife to bring out all the soft materials in his house and lay them out in his compound. When he jumped from the sky, he would have a soft and safe landing.

The bird that took the message to his wife forgot the exact instructions he had been given. He told Tortoise's wife to bring out all the hard materials in the house and lay them out in the compound. When Tortoise looked down from his very high altitude, the distance was too far. He could not make out exactly what his wife had brought out in their compound.

When it appeared to him all was set, he let go and jumped. He was dizzy and light-headed, and it took some time before he finally crash-landed. His shell was shattered. Fortunately for him, there was a great medicine man in his village at that time. The wife sent for the medicine man. He was able with his skill to patch together the shattered shell. The medicine man's fine workmanship, however, could not restore the shell as it was originally. That is why Tortoise has a rough shell.

His wife asked him what happened to the wings given to him by the birds before they left. "They took back the feathers they lent me," said Tortoise.

"You must have done something bad for the birds to take back the feathers they gave to you," said his wife.

"I was selfish," said Tortoise.

"Learn to share. It is a good thing to share," said his wife.

Wresting was another childhood pastime we enjoyed as much as storytelling. For some, it was a demonstration of their physical prowess. A good wrestler was respected. He brought honor to his community. Wrestling matches were more prevalent during the new yam festival. The festival marked the end of the farming season and harvest. It was celebrated with pomp and pageantry. There was plenty to eat and drink. Community leaders spearheaded the ceremony. The deities had to be thanked for a successful planting season and harvest. The new yam festival was a major way of expressing thankfulness and gratitude for a bountiful harvest. It can be equated to Thanksgiving in America.

The wrestling matches took place in the village square. Elders sat down on long wooden benches and talked at length about their youth and the great wrestlers of their time. While the wrestling matches were the highlight of the occasion, the music that accompanied it was a source of great joy and entertainment. The talking drum on this occasion took on a different rhythm. The sound was not that of a mere gathering of community elders for chitchat. The sound was definitely that of a wrestling match. It was unmistakable. From all corners of the community, residents knew what the sound stood for. The music floated in the air many hours before the contest started. The wrestling matches began at sunset when the heat from the sun had died down.

Spectators formed a big circle around the contestants. Boys between the ages of fourteen and sixteen opened the show, which was preliminary to the actual contest by wrestlers in their twenties. The boys had less experience than the grown-ups, but sometimes their contest was as exciting as the men's. Sometimes the boys would come up with moves that surprised and flattened their opponent on their back. Before the spectators could discern what was happening, the least-prepared wrestler was caught unaware by a fast move from his opponent, he lost his footing and balance, and was flat on his back before he knew it. The move from his opponent was so fast the looser was not able to describe what had happened to him. The crowd roared and cheered. The winner was lifted shoulder-high by people from his team and carried out of the circle.

The match between the grown-ups was more of a contest of will, strength, and endurance. The drums died down before their contest. This gave the drummers time to rest, drink some cool water, and freshen up. The wrestling teams arrived and entered the arena. The drummers had resumed their music. Spectators could see some wrestlers nodding their heads to the beat of the music. The air was charged, and the atmosphere was tense and full of expectation. Some wrestlers got really intoxicated with excitement, although some would go home disappointed by the outcome of the contest. Who would throw down the other was the big question of the evening.

A wrestler from an opposing team danced to the center of the circle. He pointed to the opponent he wished to take on. That opponent danced to where his rival stood, and they faced off. The contestants tested each other's strength by stretching out their hands and grasping the fingers of their rival. The contestant who was first in wringing free his fingers was perceived to be the stronger of the two. This was not always an accurate assessment. They then closed in on each other. Sometimes the wrestlers had different styles which led to a quick ending. In such instances, the winner turned out to be the wrestler who was smarter and quicker in outmaneuvering his opponent.

The contest was long when contestants had the same style and knew each other's moves. In this case, they would lock in on each other for minutes. Sometimes they dug their heels behind that of their opponent, but they retreated fast if they felt that was the wrong move at the particular time. Muscles all over their bodies were stretched taut, they perspired profusely, the crowd surged forward, the music from the drums added to the excitement. When the wrestling umpire felt that the contestants were evenly matched, he separated the contestants and declared the match a draw. Sometimes, however, the umpire himself was caught by a surprise move by one of the wrestlers who was hungrier for a victory. With the speed of lightning and the agility of a cat, the agile wrestler disengaged himself from his opponent, bent down fast, and caught his opponent's legs, lifted him up in the air, and flattened him on his back. Spectators roared and cheered. The chants of victory from the winner's side could be heard miles away. Spectators were elated. It was the talk of the community for many days. It was a matter of pride and honor for the victorious team.

There is a town not far from Asaba called Onitsha. The River Niger is a natural boundary between the two communities. Standing at the bank of the river at Asaba, one could see the comings and goings of people and vehicles in Onitsha. Both communities have Ibo as a common language, although with slightly different accents. Onitsha is a very busy place. It houses a large market. All sorts of wares, both domestic and foreign, are sold there. Before the erection of the Niger Bridge, passengers were ferried across the river for commercial undertakings. The Onitsha market is reputed to be one of the biggest in the whole of West Africa, a vast region made up of several countries. Some of these countries are Anglophone. Others are Francophone. The Anglophone countries were colonized by the British and have English as their official language. The Francophone nations had French colonizers, and they speak French in schools and offices. That is the official language. Presently in many West African countries, you will find people who are fluent in both English and French. The two languages are taught in institutions of higher learning.

When we were growing up, Asaba was a relatively quiet town, not a very busy place. Here and there, bushes could be found dotting the landscape and forming a sort of boundary between homes. At the outskirts of town, there were forest with massive trees stretching high into the sky as if seeking an audience with the heavenly bodies. We were serenaded by singing birds in the morning and at dusk when the birds retired for the night. All that has changed. The forest and gigantic iroko trees are gone. They have given way to modern office buildings and residential homes. Urbanization has swallowed up the once-pristine surroundings. The singing birds have been driven far into the wild.

Asaba is now the capital of Delta State. Nigeria is divided into states for administrative purposes. Asaba is no longer the sleepy town it once was. It is now a terminus, the hub for various activities. The town's origin can be traced to three ancestral lineages. Modern Asaba history, though, is linked to an illustrious son named Nnebisi. Ibo is the local language spoken, although there are many residents of Asaba with different dialects. Since its inception as a state capital, Asaba's population has grown tremendously. Asaba is both an administrative capital and an academic center. During the colonial era, Asaba was the capital of the southern protectorate of Nigeria. The town housed the Royal Niger Company set up by the British to handle trade and the exportation of raw materials to England.

Nigeria was a British colony until its independence in 1960. The first British missionaries, aside from seeking converts for their Christian faith, also established schools for the education of the people. The local chiefs were skeptical. They had some doubts about the schools built by the missionaries. When we were kids, a story was told to us by our elders of how when the first missionaries established schools, clan chiefs sent their servants to the new schools and kept their own children at home. When later, the former servants became court clerks and interpreters earning livable wages, the clan chiefs blamed themselves for their own shortsightedness.

The first appearance of the white man in the African hinterland was met with a mixture of uneasiness and suspicion. People in the hinterland had heard tales of some of the wonders performed by the white man in bigger places. They had heard the news of some of the illnesses the white man was able to cure with the medicine he brought from his country. The missionaries' journey into the hinterland, though, was unexpected. The clan chiefs and their subjects were suspicious. They had doubts about the presence of the missionaries in their midst. They consulted the priestesses of the clan. The priestesses, in turn, consulted the oracles. The message from the oracles, as far as the clans were concerned, was not good. The oracles revealed incisive changes in the clans and that sons and daughters of the clans would be carried away across the sea to distant lands. An ominous reference to the transatlantic slave trade, hence the very cautious approach toward the early missionaries by the clan chiefs.

As a kid, I admired medical doctors. I was always happy to see somebody I knew recover from an illness. I knew doctors had a role to play in the recovery. I had the ambition to become a medical doctor when I grew up. I was impressed by their healing of the sick. When I started my high school education, I discovered that I did not possess the aptitude for science subjects that would lead me to medicine. On the other hand, my English teachers loved my essays and were impressed. When we were asked to check out the meaning of words in the dictionary during English classes, 90 percent of the time, I was one of three students who came up first with the result of the search. One of my English teachers told me that I might have a future as an English teacher or in journalism. He added that how far I would go depended on how much I was willing to drive myself.

After high school, I had a three-year stint as a traveling salesman, selling baby products for a marketing company that had its headquarters in Lagos,

Nigeria's commercial capital. I was based in Kano, an ancient and industrial town in northern Nigeria. From Kano, I traveled to places such as Zaria, the seat of Ahmadu Bello University, the first institution of higher learning in Northern Nigeria. The university was named after a powerful and influential politician in postcolonial Nigeria. Ahmadu Bello can be equated to the charismatic Huey Long of Louisiana. Like Huey Long, Ahmadu Bello was a kingmaker. From Zaria, my next port of call was Kaduna, an army garrison during the Second World War. I then proceeded to Jos, Sokoto, and Maiduguri, all of them commercial centers in northern Nigeria, before returning to Kano.

I traveled along with a company driver during my sales tour. His name was Mallam Yaro, a Hausa man. The Hausas are one of the major tribes in Nigeria. The Ibos and the Yoruba come under this category too. The Yoruba are a mixture of Christians and Muslims, the Ibos are predominantly Christians, and the Hausas are largely Muslims. They inhabit the northern part of Nigeria. Mallam Yaro was a tall gentle and light-skinned man who was very religious. He was soft-spoken and full of wisdom. Despite our sometimes-hectic schedule, he found time for his prayers. A practicing Muslim is expected to pray five times each day, facing the east.

The differences in our age were immense, and I respected Mallam Yaro, who was a father figure to me. A reliable man, he always kept his word. My job as a traveling salesman called for orderliness, cleanliness, and punctuality. Customers were not to be kept waiting. Orders had to arrive on time and in good condition or the manager would say something to me about my tardiness. Doing my job well was one way of staying out of trouble.

Occasionally we had to cope with some stress, but overall, I liked the job. I liked traveling, and my sales job took me to different places. It was based on salary and commission, which gave me a handsome paycheck monthly. However, I wanted to further my education. Asaba, my hometown, is a place where education is very much cherished. Kids are encouraged to go to school and lead productive life. While I was in high school, one Mr. Ibe from my hometown returned from Canada after some years as a student in that country. He spoke in glowing terms of the advantages of studying abroad, the modern teaching and learning tools that make studying less arduous. Mr. Ibe got a good government job, a car, and an apartment. He was living well. That image was embedded in my memory, and I resolved that one day I would go abroad to seek the Golden Fleece.

COMING TO AMERICA

Nigeria is an energy-producing country. The nation produces oil and is a member of OPEC, the Organization of the Petroleum Exporting Countries. A large percentage of Nigeria's revenue comes from oil. The oil boom of the 1970s and early 1980s had a very positive impact on the country's economy. Unemployment was low, the living standard was appreciable, and many families were content with their lot.

Youths from different parts of Nigeria saw the buoyant economy as an incentive, an opportunity to further their education. Applications to institutions of higher learning soared, lots of Nigerians left for Britain, the United States of America, and Canada for higher studies. In Kano, where I was stationed, there was a United States Information Service (USIS) office. Occasionally, there were movies shown and lectures given by the personnel of the office about life in the United States and information for prospective students wishing to study in America. I visited the office regularly, read books and lots of magazines, and I gathered information about schools in the United States. I applied to several institutions for admission. Oklahoma State University, in Stillwater, was one of the institutions that offered me admission. I had an uncle schooling in Chickasha, Oklahoma, which influenced my decision to come to Oklahoma. I was excited the day I got my student visa to Oklahoma State University. I had fulfilled the pledge I made to myself some years earlier. I was coming to America the beautiful, the champion of the underdog, the beacon of hope for the downtrodden, a nation that values the differences among its people.

I got my visa a few days before Christmas in 1980. I was to start school in January 1981. I would be a freshman in the spring semester. My senior brother asked me to wait until after Christmas before leaving. I was so excited I told him that I had witnessed lots of Christmases in Nigeria and that I was eager to see what Christmas looked like in America. I boarded a plane in Lagos in December 1980 for Amsterdam, Holland, en route to Oklahoma. I was on board KLM, the Dutch airline. We were shown movies on board, and we were well-fed. We ate with spoons, forks, and knives made of real silver as opposed to the plasticware given to passengers on today's airlines. The sky was safe then. There was no fear of terrorism. There was no worry our plane would be hijacked and turned into a missile by some mischievous fellows. The flight attendants handed us Christmas greeting cards and asked us to fill them out with the addresses of our loved ones, adding that the cards would be posted in Amsterdam. Some weeks later, in Stillwater, I had forgotten about the postcard I filled out on the plane, when a postman handed me a letter from my senior brother in Nigeria, confirming the reception of a Christmas greeting card from the Dutch airline on my behalf. I was delighted. It is nice to know some organizations keep their promises.

We arrived in Amsterdam safely after a long flight. For us passengers whose final destination was not Holland, we were kept in a hotel for the night. The next day, we left Amsterdam for Chicago's O'Hare Airport. I was in for a surprise when we got to Chicago. When our plane landed, the sky was sunny. In Africa, when the sun is out, the weather is warm. As we alighted from the plane, the air was very chilly I couldn't believe what I was experiencing. I walked fast to get out of the open space which was quite chilly and get into the waiting area for passengers in transit where it was warm. I noticed too that it got dark early. These were characteristics of winter I later came to know. Different regions of the world have peculiar climatic conditions.

OKLAHOMA

After our plane landed in Chicago, we had to wait for some hours for a connecting flight to Oklahoma City. On the plane that took us to Oklahoma City, I sat beside a gentleman named Tom. He was coming back from a business trip to Asia. After formal introductions, Tom asked me:

"Do you live in Oklahoma City?"

"No, I am a foreign student. I am on my way to Oklahoma State University in Stillwater," I said.

"What country are you coming from?" Tom asked.

"I am from Nigeria," I said. He was curious. He had heard so much about the political turmoil in Africa.

"Is Nigeria under a military ruler?" he asked.

"No, Nigeria is not governed by a military government," I told him.

"Tell me more about your country," Tom said.

"Nigeria is governed by a civilian administration headed by Alhaji Shehu Shagari. It is the most populous country in Africa. Nigeria produces oil and is a member of OPEC," I told him.

"I have heard of OPEC," said Tom. "I have a friend who works for an oil company in Tulsa, Oklahoma. Often, he talks about crude oil and price fixation by OPEC," he added. "Are there rich families with oil wells in Nigeria?" Tom asked me.

"No, the oil wells are controlled by the federal government," I said.

"Is the oil revenue distributed equitably amongst the people?" Tom went on. I wasn't quite sure what he meant exactly. I followed up with a question of my own.

"What exactly do you mean?" I asked him.

"Is there fairness in the way the oil revenue is distributed since it is controlled by the government? For example, oil comes from land in some places. The land is supposed to be owned by somebody. Is there a compensation given to the people who own those areas where the oil wells are located?" Tom asked me.

I had to think about his question for a few minutes. When I was a traveling salesman in Kano, I had a friend from Port Harcourt, the capital of Rivers State. Port Harcourt is also the administrative and operational base for some oil companies located in Nigeria. Occasionally, my friend did speak about the pollution and damage caused by drilling by the oil companies. Some farmlands and fish habitats were adversely affected. There were disputes between the oil companies and the local farmers. If the farmers were compensated or not, I did not know. I decided not to bring in the issue of the disgruntled farmers.

"I do not know how the oil revenue is distributed. Right now, the Nigerian economy is doing well. Workers were given a raise not too long ago. The country is peaceful, which I think is a reflection of the people's satisfaction with the status quo," I said.

"Here in America, there are government lands with oil in it, but there are also privately owned lands with oil too. Some of the families are very rich," Tom said.

Our plane landed at night in Oklahoma City. Tom helped me to a motel and gave me information about the Greyhound bus service to Stillwater. I thanked hIm and wished him a Merry Christmas and a happy new year. In my motel room, I was fascinated by the choice of channels provided by cable television. This was not the case in Nigeria. In December 1980, when I was leaving the country, television viewers had access only to programs offered by federal or state-owned television stations. There were no twenty-four-hour television programs. Most television stations as of 1980 in Nigeria closed down for the day at about 11:00 or 11:30 p.m. It is a long way from 1980. Times have changed. Today, satellite television provides a wide variety of programs to the rich and middle class in Nigeria. Subscribers can choose from a number of service providers for their entertainment needs for a monthly fee.

I liked watching British-style wrestling when I was in Nigeria. After watching American wrestling for an hour, I went to bed. I slept sparingly, due mostly to fatigue from the long flight. My body clock was yet to adjust to my new geographical zone. I got out of bed a few minutes past eight, I showered, and put on fresh clothes. I was hungry. I wanted something to eat. I went to the motel reception office and inquired if there was a place nearby where I could get breakfast. I was told Hardee's fast-food restaurant was around the corner. I walked to Hardee's and ordered breakfast.

"What exactly do you want to eat?" asked the female attendant.

I stared at the menu she pointed to. Many of the items were unfamiliar to me.

"I am new to the country. Would you help me make a choice?" I implored.

"Where are you from?" she asked.

"I am from Nigeria," I said.

"Where is Nigeria?" she asked.

"In West Africa," I said. I was captivated by the attendant's questions and her inquiring mind.

"What kind of food do you have in Nigeria?" she further asked.

"We have different kinds of food such as yam, plantain, rice, and beans," I said.

"Oh yeah! I have seen plantain. I have tasted it. I have a Jamaican friend who likes plantain. Welcome to America," she said.

"Thank you," I replied.

When I got my breakfast tray, I gathered from my receipt that I was served sausages, eggs and biscuits, hash brown, and coffee. My breakfast before coming to America consisted of rice and beans with stew and meat, sometimes fried plantain and beans with stew, along with hot cocoa. My breakfast at Hardee's was warm and delicious. I enjoyed it. I thanked the attendant and walked back to my motel room. I packed my things and checked out. I took a taxi cab to the Greyhound bus station in downtown Oklahoma City.

After purchasing my ticket, I boarded the bus for Stillwater. When we got to Stillwater, I was offered a ride to Oklahoma State University. School was closed for the holidays. I was introduced to a Nigerian graduate student from Calabar. We drove in his car to his one-bedroom apartment which he shared with his girlfriend. With his help, I was introduced to another Nigerian fellow named Mr. Odiachi who had room for me to stay with him and his family. He had a wife and an eighteen-month-old son. Mr. Odiachi's two-bedroom apartment was within walking distance of the university campus. I could get to class easily.

There was a community of Nigerian students in Stillwater. I was not surprised by the number, but I did not know any of them before getting there. Given that desire for learning, the desire to better oneself, the ardor burning in many Nigerian youths to seek a brighter future, their presence in Stillwater was only a confirmation of something I already knew.

After the Christmas and New Year festivities, classes began in Stillwater. I had been out of school for some time, I had to readjust to constant reading. I took a light load. Stillwater was a fairly large campus, and the student body was sizable. There were students from all over the world. I had two morning classes. I had seen snow in American movies in Nigeria, but Stillwater was the place I experienced snow firsthand. One Monday morning during the spring semester of 1981, I was hurrying to class. I woke up late. I had forgotten to set my alarm clock before going to bed. It was cold, I was dressed in white pants, I had a black sweater and a black winter coat on. I was wearing black winter boots. I had no backpack. I held my books in my hands, and my pens were in my winter jacket. It had snowed the night before. Sidewalks were treacherous. There were ice patches after the snowfall. As I hurried along, I slipped on an ice patch and fell down. It seemed as if I was wrestled to the ground by a ferocious opponent. Memories of the wrestling matches I watched as a boy came rushing back. I lost my balance completely. My books were scattered all over the snow. My clothes were soaked. I was already late for class. I did not want to go back to our apartment and change my clothes, so I proceeded to class with wet clothes and books. As soon as I stepped into class, my disheveled appearance caught the attention of everybody. The instructor asked me, "What happened to you?"

"I slipped and fell down while hurrying to class," I said. My classmates had a good laugh.

"Does it snow where you came from?" asked a fellow student.

"No, it doesn't snow in Nigeria," I said.

"You will remember this experience for quite some time," said the instructor.

"I think you are right," I said to him. What I got out of my perseverance was that I made an A in the class, and I made the students' honor roll my first semester.

While in Stillwater, I was told that there were three Asaba students at the University of Central Oklahoma in Edmond. The Nigerian student who gave me the information wanted to know if I was really from Asaba town.

"Are you actually from Asaba?" he asked me.

"Yes," I said to him. "I am a full-fledged Asaba man, my father and mother are both from Asaba, I was born in Asaba, I had my elementary schooling in Asaba," I added.

He then gave me the phone number of one of the Asaba students in Edmond. As the saying goes, it is a small world. The student turned out to be a childhood friend whom I had not seen for over twelve years. It was a joyous reunion. We talked about the old days, and he told me that in addition to himself, there were four Asaba students in Edmond. He suggested that I transfer to Edmond at the end of the semester. He said that since I was new in the country, Asaba students would provide support and camaraderie. I remembered the circle of friends we had while growing up, the value we placed on our friendships, and the help we rendered to one another. I agreed with his proposal. I transferred to the University of Central Oklahoma at the end of the spring semester in 1981. I lived in Oklahoma City and commuted to school in Edmond.

Oklahoma became the forty-sixth state in the union in 1907. The nickname "Sooners" came about as a result of those who beat the gun in the land rush of 1889. A large number of people, old and young, hitched their wagon to the dream of free land when the United States government announced that Oklahoma's Indian territory would be opened for settlement. Many people had the notion of making some fortune by grabbing land and reselling it later for some profit. Boomtowns went up overnight. The territory was wild though. On the wide prairie, hopes blossomed for some. For others, their dreams died with the crack of gunfire. Gradually, the lawless and rugged frontier was tamed. Agriculture, oil, and industry are the mainstay of Oklahoma's economy.

While school was in session in Edmond, I tried to balance my classes with my job as an orderly at Bone & Joint Hospital in downtown Oklahoma City. Bone & Joint is an orthopedic hospital, one of the finest in the state. It is close to Saint Anthony's hospital, across the street. There is an underground tunnel linking both hospitals. We used to take patients on a gurney through the tunnel for tests at Saint Anthony's. We left the patients there with the lab technicians. They called us when they were done testing, and we came and took the patients back to Bone & Joint. I was privileged to work at Bone & Joint. I made some good friends. I was told that it is the cream of the crop among medical students who go in for heart, brain, and orthopedic surgery. That is where the money is in medicine, I was told. The doctors and nurses at Bone & Joint Hospital were friendly to both patients and employees. It was a friendly environment. I enjoyed my stay at Bone & Joint Hospital.

My classes in Edmond were mostly in the mornings. When I was scheduled to work at the hospital, it was usually in the evenings. I took a few summer classes. These were usually fast-paced. I had to work twice as hard during the summer sessions, which was not the case for me during regular semesters. During the summer sessions I did not go to school,

I worked two jobs. I used the money for traveling, sometimes within the United States, at other times, abroad. My former job as a traveling salesman in Nigeria got me interested in visiting different places, learning about people and their culture.

Football is big in Oklahoma. Oklahomans are enthusiastic about football, college or professional. To add to their enthusiasm, Oklahoma University in Norman (OU) has done the state proud by winning the national college football championship a number of times. Having been reared in Nigeria where soccer is the dominant sport, American football did not appeal to me initially. I saw it as a bunch of guys knocking each other down and at other times, scrambling for the ball. My supervisor at Bone & Joint Hospital taught me the rules of the game. After tutoring me about American football, I came to appreciate the strategy, the teamwork, the execution behind every move on the field. It was a game in which each team used not only their physical ability but also their brains to outsmart their opponent. I got interested in both college and professional football. I watched with keen interest as coach Jimmy Johnson took over the Dallas Cowboys. Before his arrival, the Cowboys were performing poorly. They were one of the lowest-ranked teams in the National Football League before the arrival of Jimmy Johnson. Patiently and steadily, Coach Johnson turned the team around. It took some time though. The Dallas

Cowboys started winning matches. There were some doubting Thomases. Some football critics maintained that the Cowboys had not been tested. They were only playing against weak teams, the critics maintained. The San Francisco 49ers were one of the hottest teams in the National Football League in 1993. To add to the authenticity of the Dallas Cowboys, it was a home game for the 49ers. The Cowboys had to go to San Francisco for the game. The Cowboys went to San Francisco and took care of business. They beat the 49ers on their home turf. The critics were silenced. The Dallas Cowboys under Coach Jimmy Johnson were for real. They were to be taken seriously. They deserved some respect. The Cowboys won the Super Bowl back to back in 1993 and 1994. I was very impressed. I have been a football fan since then.

As a liberal arts student, French was one of the subjects I took in Edmond. Fortunately for me, I had some background in French. I took some French classes in high school. I was pretty good with my written work, less so in the oral part of the class. My instructor in French in Edmond was a slim and pretty lady. She told the class funny stories about her student days and her travels in France. She had been to a number of European countries. Her knowledge of Africa, though, was limited. She was surprised by my performance on our first test. I got 95 percent. She was one of those teachers who liked pacing the front of the class while she was talking to her students. She was a fine dresser. The female students in the class talked at length after classes about her fabulous outfits. The male students talked about her gorgeous figure. The Monday after our first test, she walked into the class, placed her books on the instructor's table, stood in front of the class for a few seconds, and called, "John Keshi." I stood up. With a smile on her face, she said, "Sit down." I sat down. "Where are you from?" she asked.

"I am from Nigeria," I said.

"That is in Africa," she followed up.

"That is correct," I said to her.

"Do you study French in school in Africa?" she went on.

"Yes, we do. It is not a compulsory subject, but students who have a flair for languages take it up," I said to her.

"I see from your test paper that you have a good background in the subject," she said.

"I like the class, but I am not good with the oral part of it," I told her.

"Practice, practice, practice. You will get better," she said to me.

I worked hard. I got an A at the end of the semester.

The months of May and June are graduation time. Four years of hard work culminates into college degrees. Term paper deadlines, back-to-back tests from various classes, putting long hours into test preparations were behind us. We were looking forward to our graduation and diploma. It was time for joy and celebration. Graduation parties were common at this time of year in Oklahoma City and environs. Weeks of good planning usually resulted in successful graduation parties. Graduating students were presented with gifts by friends and well-wishers. The size and number of presents a graduating student got, depended on how wide his or her circle of friends were. Friends and relatives from faraway places were present at the graduation ceremony, all dressed up in beautiful and bright clothing for the august occasion.

A day or two before the party, some graduating students went to the countryside, to outlying towns near Oklahoma City, to buy a goat. The goat was slaughtered in the country, and the meat was brought back to the city. It was used for the preparation of stew. Goat meat is a delicacy in Nigeria. On the day of the party, food and drinks were plentiful. Some graduating students gave speeches, expressing their gratitude to the instructors and librarians who contributed to their success. Music and dancing added to the merrymaking. The chief celebrant opened the floor to dancing with a partner. Invitees joined in with partners as well. Food and drinks were replenished as needed. The celebration sometimes lasted into the wee hours of the morning. Out-of-town relatives and friends leave after the graduation ceremony.

The celebrations were over, we were done with partying, our student days were behind us. It was time to face the real world.

"Life is like a box of chocolates. You never know what you're gonna get" (*Forrest Gump*).

There are uncertainties in life, sometimes surprises. Some of the surprises have a happy ending, others heartbreaking. It is not what happened to us that decides our fate. The ultimate outcome sometimes hinges on the way and manner we react to what happened to us. Though we cannot control what people say, we can control our reaction to what was said. With maturity and self-discipline, we can lighten the burden life sometimes places on our path.

NORTHERN CALIFORNIA

The years following my graduation were not easy ones. After some difficulties and setbacks, my path led me to Santa Rosa in Northern California. When I arrived in Santa Rosa in October 1998, I had just dropped out of a nursing program in Anaheim, Southern California. I was broke, I needed to make a living, so I went in search of a job. A few days after submitting my application, Primrose, an assisted living facility, called me for an interview. Two days after my interview with the facility manager, he called me and told me I had been offered a job. I was at Primrose until January 1999 when I received another job offer from Creekside Rehabilitation and Behavioral Health, also located in Santa Rosa. The pay was slightly higher, and I had more hours, so I decided to take the job offer.

During my sojourn as a nursing student, I had worked in hospitals and skilled nursing facilities in Southern California. When I got to Creekside, I learned quickly that working in a mental health facility called for more patience than was required in hospitals and other health centers.

Mental health services in Nigeria, where I was born, is still in its infancy. It is a world away from what is available here in America. Some people tend to avoid the mentally ill even when they are not violent. The stigma attached to mental illness is one reason for this pathetic condition. In some communities, the mentally ill are looked upon as possessed by an evil spirit. Exorcism to cast out the evil spirit by a local medicine man may be recommended in such places. In other instances, spiritual churches get involved in seeking a cure for the mentally ill. Fasting and prayers are embarked upon for some period of time by groups within the church. The purification of body and soul leads to salvation, adherents of these churches contend. Sometimes the person involved in the intercession emerges from his or her torments a new man or woman. He or she is asked to "go forth and sin no more." Although the impact of these faith healers is limited, their services are sometimes effective.

A short introduction to Creekside

The center was a long-term mental health facility. Patients were referred to as residents. Their stay ranged from a few months to over a year in some cases. The center catered to the mentally ill and people with substance abuse and alcohol problems. The well-being of the residents was the responsibility of the nursing department. The rehabilitation arm of Creekside had the task of providing the residents with coping skills to enable them to get back into society after their release from the center. Classes such as cooking were among some of the skills taught to the residents by the rehabilitation department.

One of the highlights of the teachings the rehabilitation department imparted to residents was the message of hope. The wish, the longing that through some earnest and meaningful efforts, tomorrow can be better than today. The message that we can learn from our mistakes and move on with our lives. Through some conscious efforts, pessimism can give way to optimism. We can say yes to life after some setbacks or drawbacks. Residents were urged to muster their inner strength and look forward to a new beginning, live one day at a time, and interact positively with their community. On the part of the community into which the residents go back into, they were urged to lend a helping hand in the recovery process of residents by a show of friendship and tolerance. This acceptance and positive attitude eliminated the shame some residents experienced after their departure from Creekside.

Most of the residents at Creekside mental health center came from Sonoma County. The program was headed by a clinical director. Mental health workers conducted rounds every fifteen minutes. The rounds were designed to ascertain resident location in the facility and what he or she was doing at that point in time.

When I came on board in January 1999, I was hired as a mental health worker. My duties included ensuring that residents under my care took their showers, went for their meals and medications, and attended designated programs. For the low-functioning residents in my group, I assisted them with showers, laundry, and keeping their rooms orderly. My job description made me a caregiver.

On a bright and sunny day in April, Adolfo was admitted to Creekside. He was five feet six inches tall, slim, and had the paleness and unkemptness of someone underfed and living in the street. Adolfo was abusing street drugs. He was confused and disoriented and going through the agony of withdrawal. He urinated on himself and defecated on his bed. The odor coming from Adolfo's room was sharp and repulsive. The mental health worker assigned to Adolfo was loathe to help him. He pretended he was busy. I felt Adolfo's caregiver was reluctant to help him because of the bad odor, the filthy room, and the mess the resident himself was in. For a caregiver who took his responsibilities seriously, Adolfo's condition wouldn't have mattered. He would have gone in to render the necessary help. He did not do that. Adolfo needed immediate assistance. The charge nurse on duty and myself stepped in and helped. We took Adolfo to the shower room, washed him with soap and water, dried him with towels, and put fresh clothes on him. I cleaned and sanitized his room and put fresh sheets on his bed. Adolfo laid down. Three hours later, Adolfo was soiled again. This time, the mental health worker assigned to Adolfo claimed he was on dinner break. I was saying to myself, *was this guy vetted before he was given a job here?* If he was not ready to handle situations such as this, why was he given a job in this facility? I told the charge nurse that the attitude of Adolfo's mental health worker left much to be desired and that she should talk to him. I wondered how one could be so indifferent, how one could be so coldhearted as to have no feeling for the suffering of a resident. Instead of helping a confused and disoriented person, he chose to walk away. It was a case of utter lack of compassion and abandonment of one's responsibility. It was a shameless display of a poor work ethic, to say the least.

I read somewhere in a Christian magazine that by sharing people's problem, you make their burden lighter. It doesn't take much to make a difference in somebody's life. The willingness, openheartedness, and kindness have to be there though. These virtues were lacking in Adolfo's mental health worker. He was just there to collect a paycheck, a paycheck that, one could argue, he did not earn. I took Adolfo to the shower room. I washed him with water, soap, and a wash cloth. I dried him with a towel and put another set of fresh clothes on him. I changed his soiled sheets with fresh ones, and he laid down.

Two weeks later, the effects of the street drugs he was taking had worn off. Adolfo approached me and asked, "Are you John?"

"Yes, I am John," I answered.

"Thank you very much. I was told you helped me when I was disoriented," he said.

"The charge nurse and myself helped you the first time. The second time, I handled the situation by myself," I replied.

"I appreciate your help, John," Adolfo added.

I was deeply touched by his comments.

"You are welcome, Adolfo. This is what we are here for," I said to him.

As time progressed and his mental status improved, Adolfo opened up. His father grew up in New York and schooled there before moving to San Francisco where he got a job as a salesman selling scientific instruments. His father met his mother in San Francisco, and they got married. The early years were pleasant. The young couple settled down and started a family. According to Adolfo, his father was a neat and well-dressed man who placed emphasis on tidiness. After waking up, the beds had to be made. Unclean dishes in the sink disgusted him. Disorderliness represented a failure, and procrastination was a lazy man's excuse. Adolfo's father could not stand a messy house. His mother did her best to keep their home tidy and well organized.

Adolfo's father was doing well with his job. He was making good money. The company his father was working for started expanding. With expansion came more responsibility for his father. He started traveling. Sometimes for days, he was away from home. Since there was enough money to take care of the family, his mother did not complain initially about his father's absences from home. Trouble began when Adolfo's father started keeping late nights when he was in town. When he got home, he had no appetite for food and retired to bed. He seldom showed up for Adolfo's sporting events at school when he was in town. Simple questions from his mother to his father gave rise to heated arguments. Adolfo's mother suspected his father was having an affair, but she needed strong evidence to back up her suspicions.

Things came to a head one day when Adolfo and his mother cut short their visit to his grandparents' and returned home a day earlier than planned. As his mother opened the door to their home and they got in, they heard shuffles coming from the bedroom. As they moved closer, they heard muffled voices coming from the bedroom. Adolfo's mother knocked on the bedroom door. There was no response. She banged on the door. "Open the door, Alex. Your game is over!" she yelled. After a few minutes of hesitation, the key to the bedroom door turned, and the door opened. Adolfo's father was in front of the door with his pants on, bare-chested. There was a woman with a frightened look on her face behind him. Adolfo's mother could not contain her rage. She went straight for Adolfo's father and started hitting him. His mistress ran out of the house barefooted, leaving her footwear behind. The fight that ensured between Adolfo's parents was bitter and destructive. When it was over, the bedroom was a wreck. Adolfo's mother felt betrayed. All those years she tried very hard to be a good wife, kept their house homely, and stayed faithful to her husband, she felt, was taken for granted. The mother was so disgusted she did not want anything to do with the house anymore. She filed for divorce a few days after the incident and moved out. Things were never the same again for Adolfo. His relationship with his father became strained. He lost faith in his dad. His father continued with his travels and hired a live-in housemaid. But she could never replace a mother. Things were obviously different for Adolfo.

He started skipping school and hanging out with the wrong crowd. He smoked marijuana and graduated to harder drugs in an effort to ease pain and take away boredom. While in the street, his highest goal was how to get the next fix. When he got home, he argued bitterly with the housekeeper.

When Adolfo's father came back from one of his sales tours, he was shocked by the pathetic condition he saw his son in. Adolfo had lost a lot of weight. He was confused and in a druggy haze. Adolfo's father was overcome by guilt, fear, and embarrassment. He picked up the phone and started inquiring where his son could get help, and he was directed to Creekside.

Charge Nurse Peggy was raised in the East. For a change of scenery, she moved West to California. She was a plump woman with average height, an oval-shaped face, and almond-shaped eyes. On her good days, she could be likened to a happy mother who ensured her kids were well-fed and had taken their medication. On the other hand, she could be strict depending on the prevailing condition at the center. Charge Nurse Peggy was an efficient nurse, and she took her job seriously. One afternoon, she called me to the conference room where she was taking her break.

"Sit down, John. I have been impressed by the good comments coming from the residents about you. You would make a good nurse. Why did you drop out of the nursing school in Anaheim?" she asked

"It is a long story, Peggy. I get unhappy and emotional recalling my nursing school days. It is like reopening an old wound. I would rather not talk about it," I said to her.

"Okay, John, I am sorry. Would you help Raul with his shower?"

"Yes, I will help him."

"Thank you, John."

"You are welcome, Peggy."

Raul was a tall guy, six feet five inches, from a good working-class family. His parents were devout Christians. Every Sunday, his mother took the family to church, where she played the organ.

Raul took to sports as a youngster. Even in grade school, his athletic ability was evident. He loved basketball and was good at it. He played for his high school team where he contributed immensely to many winning matches. He was outstanding for his three-point shots. Several hours every week after school, the school basketball coach made sure his players spent some time in the school gymnasium, conditioning themselves and practicing. Basketball greats Julius Erving (Dr. J) and Wilt Chamberlain were his heroes. In his spare time, Raul watched videos of their great performances on the basketball court. He had dreams of going to college to play basketball and, with some luck, going professional after college.

It all changed with an ugly and unfortunate car accident one night in June on his way back from a graduation party. A drunken driver ran a red light and slammed into the vehicle Raul and his friend were riding in as his friend was about to negotiate a turn. Both vehicles were totaled. They were damaged beyond repair. Raul and his friend were semi-conscious when the ambulance arrived. The medical emergency technicians had to pry the car open and pull Raul and his friend out. The drunken driver was pronounced dead on arrival at the hospital. Raul's friend was paralyzed from the waist down. Raul had his right leg broken, and his knee was torn. Raul was in the hospital for a long time. After hospitalization came therapy. Even after therapy, Raul did not fully regain the use of his right leg. He walked with a limp. The doctor told him his basketball ambitions were behind him and that he should think of something else to do with his life. For Raul, it was devastating news. For him, it seemed as if a dagger was thrust into his heart. For days, he lay on his bed and did not come out from his room, refusing contact with family members and friends. The gap between his dreams and the reality of his situation seemed to have triggered the onset of his depression. Raul started drinking and using drugs. His depressive mood turned suicidal. He smashed the television set in his room. He poked himself with sharp objects, he ranted all night, his mood swings were wild. Raul was considered a danger to himself and to others. There was worry and concern in his family about him. Upon the recommendation of a psychiatrist, he was moved to Creekside.

Safety at Creekside was considered vital to the smooth running of the center. To this end, twice annually, a program called PART, Professional Assault Response Training, was organized. Staff were taught how to diffuse difficult situations involving residents without serious injury to residents or staff. Just like with every rule, there is an exception, and this method was not 100 percent foolproof. It was like boot camp on a minor scale. Physical fitness was emphasized. The instructor fired off orders like a drill sergeant. This time, however, participants were not going to a war front. The war could be right there at Creekside, dealing with truculent residents. Sometimes, the situation did get ugly. When it did happen, we had to put up with it. It was part of the job. Occasionally though, some sissy members of staff did complain.

For the two days PART was organized, it was held in the small dining room. The small dining room was reserved for residents on special diets, like diabetics. There was a second dining room, called the large dining room, for residents on regular diets. When PART was in session, all residents congregated in the large dining room for breakfast and lunch. The large dining room was square-like in shape, with long tables and chairs on opposite sides of the room. There were no fixed sitting patterns. Residents could sit anywhere they chose.

Josh, the oldest male mental health worker, was the self-appointed leader. Josh did not believe in a medium. He lived largely and sometimes took things to extreme. He was above-average height, and he had broad shoulders, thinning hair, a pointed nose, and a slow gait. Josh dressed casually, mostly jeans and T-shirts. He liked country music and loved to eat. He ate anything as long as it did not upset his stomach. Josh enjoyed the company of women who liked sex and would take care of him. He was a gigolo, always moving from one girlfriend to another. He bragged about the number of women he had taken to bed. "Conquests" was the term he used for his former girlfriends.

During lunch one afternoon while PART was in session, Josh and I were supervising the residents. Sometimes, there were surplus rations. When it was available, staff was allowed to eat it. There was a surplus ration at this point in time, and Josh took it. There were vacant seats in the large dining room. Josh chose to stand up while eating, his face toward the wall, his back to the residents he was supposed to be supervising.

"John, why is Josh standing up and facing the wall while eating?" asked Adolfo. "That is weird!"

"I do not know, Adolfo. That beats me," I replied.

"Hey, Josh, why are you standing up and backing us? You don't like our faces?"

The dining room reverberated with laughter.

"His jeans must be very expensive. He does not want any stain on it," said Raul.

"At least he can face us while standing," declared Adolfo.

Josh was embarrassed. He hurriedly devoured his rice and chicken and bolted out of the large dining room.

Weekends at Creekside, particularly Sundays, were managed by a skeleton staff. Administrative offices were closed. Senior management staff were not around, and the Rehabilitation Department was shut down as well. One Sunday in July, Josh took out some residents for a smoke break. This was at a patio behind the hospital building. The duration of the break was supposed to be fifteen minutes. With Sunday being a slow day and not much happening at the center, Josh arbitrarily extended the break to forty-five minutes without the permission of the charge nurse on duty. I had gone to the conference room to retrieve a magazine, and I was getting back to the nurses' station when I saw Mariam, a resident, stagger in from the smoke break area and slumped to the floor. I rushed to where she was lying.

"What is the matter, Mariam?" I asked

"I have difficulty breathing," she gasped.

She had been having stomach problems for some time. I stretched out my right hand and she grabbed onto it and I helped her up.

"Let's go talk to the charge nurse," I said to her. "Hold on to the guard rails along the wall with your left hand. I will hold your right hand," I added.

We walked slowly toward the office. At the entrance to the office, she slumped to the floor for the second time. The charge nurse on duty rushed out.

"What is the matter, Mariam?" asked the charge nurse.

She could not speak.

"Inez, John, help her to the quiet room. John, take her vital signs," the charge nurse said calmly and firmly.

We both took each arm, stood her up, and walked slowly toward the quiet room. After a few steps, Mariam's knees buckled under her, and she slumped to the floor and started vomiting. She had large emesis.

"Get a wheelchair, Inez," I said.

I bent down, went on my knees, and held on to Mariam. Inez got a wheelchair, and we both helped Mariam into it. We took her to the quiet room where she laid down. The charge nurse dialed 911 for paramedics. Oxygen was administered to Mariam. Creekside was not far from the police and fire stations. The paramedics arrived promptly. I narrated what I saw to them. Mariam was breathing, but she was not responding to questions from the paramedics. They transferred her to a gurney, attached telemetry to her, and wheeled her to their ambulance waiting at the entrance to the psychiatric hospital. She was loaded into the ambulance and taken to the hospital along with her chart for checkup and observation.

"John, what happened during the smoke break?" asked Inez.

"I don't know. I wasn't there. I was coming back from the conference room when I saw her on the floor. She has stomach problems. It could be kidney stones or stomach flu, I am not sure," I said to Inez.

"The large emesis she had and her inability to speak scared me. I hope she recovers," said Inez.

"I hope so too," I added.

Mariam was at the hospital for several hours before she was brought back to Creekside. The next day, Josh started making comments to the effect that Mariam was not sick. She was just acting out and seeking attention, he contended. Mariam was red in the face with anger, and she spoke to Charge Nurse Peggy about Josh's infuriating comments. Charge Nurse Peggy calmed her down and told her that the matter would be taken up at the next care conference meeting. Care conference was a meeting where the well-being and affairs of the residents were discussed. Sometimes among staff members; in other cases, in conjunction with medical doctors or psychiatrists who had patients at Creekside.

On Wednesday, at the care conference meeting with Dr. Joe, Charge Nurse Peggy, Mariam, and I were in attendance. Mariam brought up the "trash talk," as she put it, that Josh was spreading. Dr. Joe was a well-dressed psychiatrist of average height. He always wore custom-tailored suits with matching ties. He exhibited the maturity of someone used to dealing with people with problems.

"John, go and tell Josh I want to see him," said Dr. Joe.

I left the room and returned a few minutes later with Josh. We both sat down.

"Josh, Mariam says you are taunting her about her trip to the hospital," said Dr. Joe. "If you must know, she has problems with her stomach," he added.

"I was just kidding, Doc," said Josh.

"You don't kid with someone's health," said Dr. Joe.

"This is not the first report I am getting about your insolence towards residents, particularly females," said Charge Nurse Peggy. "Conduct yourself like the adult that you are, and behave yourself," she added.

"I want an apology, Doc," declared Mariam.

Josh's eyes flared up. He remained silent for a few seconds.

"Did you hear that, Josh?" Dr. Joe asked gently.

"I am sorry for my comments, Mariam. I will not do it again," Josh said, and he walked out of the conference room.

"Josh is something else. He is always stepping on the toes of residents," said Charge Nurse Peggy.

"He will get in trouble someday," predicted Mariam.

A few days after the care conference meeting with Dr. Joe, Mariam approached me and told me that Josh came into their room unannounced. He did not knock on their door before coming into their room while he was conducting rounds. Mariam was stark naked, and Josh did not apologize. I had observed firsthand when Josh went into a female's room without knocking on the door, so Mariam's statement did not come as a surprise to me. I reported my observation to the charge nurse on duty, and I asked Mariam to do the same thing. Josh's apology to Mariam a few days earlier during care conference, I felt, was self-serving and dishonest. His behavior in regard to his unannounced entry into female rooms was moral turpitude at its worst and barbaric.

Human beings everywhere need food for their sustenance. We would not be able to function properly without adequate nutrition. The administration at Creekside maintained the notion that human sexuality or the desire for sexual intercourse was manifested in every mature body, including those in confined environments such as Creekside. In furtherance of this idea, the center allowed sexual intimacy among consenting residents. It, however, advocated safety. Residents wishing to engage in sexual intercourse were advised to use condoms, which were available to the residents upon request.

Pete, a round-faced resident, was a tall and handsome man. He loved women and saw himself as a ladies' man. Pete was close and intimate with a female resident named Dominga. One evening, I was conducting rounds. I knocked on the door to Dominga's room, and her roommate, Anna, said, "Come in." Anna's bed was in the farther end of the room. Dominga had her bed near to the entrance to the door. When I pushed open the door, Pete was on top of Dominga. They were butt naked and were making love. Anna's curtain was drawn, and she was oblivious to the fun her roommate was having. I stepped back and closed the door. Later that evening, I took Pete aside and asked him why he did not pull Dominga's curtain before they started having fun. Pete said that with Anna's curtain drawn, they thought that was enough precaution. He added that at the instant I knocked on the door, he was ejaculating and could not help himself. I advised him against carelessness, and I urged him to exercise more discretion on future occasions.

Dominga was above-average height, with a pretty face and black hair. She abused drugs. She once lived with her cousin, but when she got pregnant and could not say who was the child's father, her cousin got angry and threw her out. The fact that she was promiscuous and had multiple sex partners angered her cousin. Due to lack of care, she had a miscarriage and lost the baby. She led a precarious life thereafter. She sometimes slept in abandoned cars or squatted in empty houses and had her meals at soup kitchens. This was when the weather was warm. When it got cold, she moved to a shelter. The shelter had a precondition. People wishing to receive help had to be clean. They had to be drug-free. Somehow in the winter, Dominga's need for warm housing surpassed the urge to get high on street drugs. She managed to stay clean and was accepted into the shelter. When she was there, she had access to warm meals, free clothing, warm water, and soap. In the street, one could hardly make her out as homeless. She blended well into a working-class group with her neat appearance and clean clothes.

It was while she was in the shelter she was introduced to a social worker who took up her case and grilled her on a number of issues. Where was she born? Dominga was born in California out of wedlock. What had she to say about her parents and early childhood? She saw her father last when she was seven, and her mother dropped her off at her grandmother's when she was ten. What sort of drugs was she taking? She was a recreational user of marijuana and crack. Was she a pusher for a dealer, or was she just an occasional user? Dominga was not a pusher. She occasionally got high on marijuana and crack with the people she hung out with. When the social worker was satisfied she could handle

Dominga's case, she filed the requisite papers that brought Dominga to Creekside. Getting her off the street and into a recovery center where professionals would handle her detoxification process was a first step toward getting her back into normal life. If detoxification was successful and she stayed clean, job training would then follow.

From the tales narrated by Dominga, the homeless came in different categories, but they all had some things in common with everybody else in society—the need for a safe place to spend the night, a meal or two that was warm each day, and for some, the companionship of another human being.

They were those down on their luck, who lost their job or were laid off and did not have the savings to pay rent. In shelters for the first time, they were sort of bewildered at the unfortunate turn of events for them. They were neatly clothed, often in their own clothes. They ate food offered to them silently, and a keen observer could detect that anxious look on their faces, as if asking themselves, *when is it going to get better?*

There were the hardcore homeless. Some were mentally ill and had been in the streets for long. They seemed to have been hardened by the difficulties they had been through. Time did not matter to them. They took in all the scenery the street offered—moving vehicles, hawkers parading various items for sale, the policeman directing traffic, a taxicab picking up a passenger. They didn't care about their appearances as long as they were not naked. Unkemptness meant nothing to them; their shoes were worn out, sometimes tattered. They spent the night wherever darkness met them—maybe a park, an abandoned house, or a broken down and forsaken vehicle, as long as the police did not ask them to leave.

Then there were those who had fallen out of favor with parents or family members and, with nowhere to turn to, end up in shelters. When the traditional shelters were full, they did not care taking up temporary shelter underneath overhead bridges that form part of the infrastructure in large cities.

These were the conventional views of the homeless in society. Dominga, however, gave another version of the homeless, less known to the public. It was a common assumption that the homeless had been rejected by wife, husband, boyfriend or girlfriend, or even family members due to irrational behavior, incompetence, drug abuse, or being too difficult to live with. This might be true in some cases, but not in every case. In some instances, it was the other way around. When it boiled down to the survival of the fittest, absolute power determined who would stay and who would leave. The person wielding power might not be a nice fellow. All that mattered at that point in time was that he or she was in a position to call the shots.

There was the case of Brenda, who shared an apartment with her boyfriend. All was well until she was in an advanced stage of her pregnancy. She was no longer available for lovemaking, she was not in the mood, and it was not a safe thing to do. Her boyfriend started cheating on her. Brenda found out through a friend that the man she shared the same roof with and the father of the child she was carrying was seeing another woman. Brenda made inquiries and provided evidence. The name of the woman her boyfriend was seeing, her place of residence and work. This led to ugly confrontations with her boyfriend. The ruckus they caused was a nuisance to neighbors. Brenda's boyfriend accused her of irrational behavior and mental illness. The landlord of the property where they lived intervened. The lease to the apartment where they lived was in the name of Brenda's boyfriend. The fact that she contributed to the payment of rent and bills did not matter. Brenda was asked to leave by the landlord. She was powerless in this case despite the arbitrariness and injustice of the decision handed out to her. To add insult to injury, Brenda's ex-boyfriend brought in the woman he was fooling around with after Brenda had moved out. Brenda herself ended up in a shelter for single and expectant mothers. Her ex-boyfriend and the landlord in this case wielded all the power.

Pete came to Creekside because of substance abuse problems. He was once the breadwinner of his family. A lover and a hilarious character, he loved the good times. Pete was nicknamed the "funny one" for his ability to make jokes out of situations. He told me his story. Pete worked for eight years for a manufacturing company. It was eight years of good living with his wife and two kids. The pay was good. The benefits were equally attractive. As the years rolled by, things started to change within the company. The cost of raw materials and production started rising. The company's profit margin began dwindling. The financial burden on the business mounted. To save the company, the board of management opted for relocation, closed down the plants, and moved production overseas where the cost of labor and production were cheaper.

Pete managed with part-time jobs for quite some time while searching for full-time employment that never materialized. With a family to support and no steady income to cope with the bills, he became depressed. Inability to care properly for his family amounted to humiliation and loss of respect from his wife. Without a steady means of earning a proper living and supporting his family as required by societal norms, he felt a debasement of his status as head of his family. Worse, he felt impotent. The forced dependency of his kids on their mother's earning, inadequate at best, was galling. His depression mounted. Pete sought relief in alcohol and drifted into hard drugs. He got hooked. He tried to hide his drug use from his wife, but she eventually found out. Pete would come home drunk, irritated, and on edge. His behavior was sometimes erratic. His wife thought that his joblessness was part of his problem. She had some suspicions though. One day she was about to launder the kids' clothes as well as Pete's. As she reached into the clothes' pockets to make sure there were empty before loading them into the washing machine, her hand met with something in Pete's pocket. She took the substance out and held on to it. She did not show it to Pete. She was not sure what it was. The rest of the day, she maintained a calm demeanor and kept her secret to herself. The next day, after Pete had gone out, she went into the neighborhood and inquired about the substance she found in her husband's pocket the previous day. She was told it was crack cocaine. Her suspicions were confirmed. When Pete came back that evening, she confronted him with her evidence. Pete could not deny it. His wife gathered his clothes in a bag and threw him out. She barred Pete from seeing their kids. The wife saw him as a bad influence and an unfit father for their kids. I wondered how Pete was able to acquire the money for his booze and drugs given the fact that he had no job. I wanted to ask him that question. On second thought, I dropped the idea. It would have amounted to reopening old wounds Pete might not be happy about. I felt it was gentlemanly to respect his feelings.

Pete, when sober and free from street drugs, was a different man. At Creekside, due to his forceful personality, he became the unofficial spokesman for the residents; sometimes challenging Charge Nurse Peggy about matters concerning the residents. Most residents at Creekside considered Charge Nurse Peggy, a fair-minded woman. Don't tell that to Pete. To him, Charge Nurse Peggy was a bad cop.

On a beautiful spring morning in March, the sun had risen from the east. On the trees that lined the creek outside the mental health center, one could hear the singing of birds. Inside Creekside, the morning routine had started. Residents were getting out of bed, showering, and getting ready for breakfast. The psychiatric technicians were getting ready with medications for the residents. Charge Nurse Peggy walked up to where I was helping a resident with his laundry and said to me, "John, when you are done, give me the names of residents who do not show up for breakfast."

"Okay, Peggy," I replied.

In the small dining room, where I was constantly, two residents did not show up for breakfast. Some residents occasionally skipped breakfast and stayed in their rooms. In this category belonged Adolfo and Pete. Later that morning, I supplied the names of the two residents who did not show up for breakfast to Charge Nurse Peggy. The next day, Tuesday, I was off duty. On my return to work on Wednesday,

I found out that more names had been taken off the breakfast list. The names taken off showed up sporadically for breakfast. They were not constant. They showed up when they felt like it. I decided to have an update on what may have transpired while I was off duty. I approached a colleague of mine named Amanda, who worked alternately in both the large and small dining rooms.

Amanda was a conscientious and cool-headed mental health worker. She was reliable and dependable. She was tall and trim, with long chestnut hair and wide blue eyes. She was never afraid to speak her mind. Amanda was raised in a Christian family where at an early age, her parents implanted in her that Christian principle of "Do unto others like you would want them do unto you." She narrated a short anecdote told to her when she was growing up.

"Let the eagle perch, let the hawk perch on the same tree. If the eagle or the hawk should refuse the other the right to perch on the tree, may the wing of the aggressor broke." The meaning of the story she concluded was "let justice and fair play reign." That was her guiding principle in life.

"Are there changes in the breakfast list in the large dining room?" I asked her.

"Some names were taken off the breakfast list in the large dining room," Amanda replied. "Some of the names taken off sometimes showed up for breakfast," she added.

"I am puzzled. I gave Charge Nurse Peggy only two names on Monday. More names have been taken off the breakfast list in the small dining room," I told Amanda.

Residents who were not present daily for breakfast but showed up occasionally came to the dining room only to discover that there was no breakfast tray for them. There were some tense moments during breakfast for some days in the dining rooms. At the nurses' station, Pete said to me, "What is going on, John? I did not get breakfast this morning. Adolfo also said he did not get breakfast. We will protest, John. Denying us breakfast is a bad idea."

"Take it easy, Pete. I will bring the matter up in our next care conference meeting," I said to him.

Some days later, at the care conference meeting, Pete beat me to it. He lashed out at Charge Nurse Peggy.

"Dr. Joe, I would like Charge Nurse Peggy to explain to me why I did not get breakfast on Wednesday."

"You did not get breakfast last Wednesday?" Dr. Joe asked as if he was not quite sure of what he heard.

"That is correct, Doc," Pete said.

"What is going on, Peggy?" asked Dr. Joe.

"The cooks tell administration that they have been throwing away lots of breakfast lately. Administration tells us to take off the breakfast list residents who do not show up for breakfast," said Charge Nurse Peggy.

"That is outrageous," blurted Pete.

"Calm down, Pete," admonished Dr. Joe.

"The residents paid for three meals. They should not be shortchanged," added Dr. Joe.

"I am just a messenger, Doc. I do not make the rules around here," said Charge Nurse Peggy.

"This is not a good policy. I will talk to the clinical director after this meeting," Dr. Joe retorted.

"Dr. Joe, there have been tense moments during breakfast lately. This is a direct result of the absence of breakfast trays for some residents," I said.

"Something has to be done real soon, John. We do not want a bigger problem on our hands," replied Dr. Joe.

A few days after this meeting, management reversed itself. It went back to supplying every resident with a breakfast tray. As Pete said earlier on, denying some residents their breakfast tray was a bad idea. If residents elected to skip a meal, that was their own business. They ought not be short-changed according to Dr. Joe. Cost-cutting measures should not be carried out at the expense of residents. Administration ought to have looked at other measures that did not involve denying some residents their breakfast.

Bernado and Rosalia were two residents at Creekside who saw themselves as tough. Bernado was short and muscle-bound, with a square face. He wore black jeans and white T-shirt often and wore his hat with the face backward. He had a big mouth and an acidic tongue and obviously was not the type that settled for a compromise.

Rosalia was Bernado's counterpart, although she would have resented any comparison. Rosalia would have contended that Bernado was more of a brawler than herself. Both were strongheaded and combatant in their own way.

There was banking at Creekside, although it was not the type of bank you would want to take your money for safekeeping. Creekside bank did not offer interest on the money kept there. That was and is still a no-no in the arena of commerce. No wise investor would go for such a banking system. Banking at Creekside was a meeting of residents and two staff from the rehabilitation department for the purpose of handing out allowances to residents. The money came from residents' respective counties. Sometimes it was from family members or friends of the residents. The only thing banking at Creekside had in common with banking in the broader community was that residents had to stand in line and take their turn.

One afternoon in September, banking was taking place in the large dining room. Bernado walked into the room for banking. Instead of getting into the line and waiting for his turn, Bernado cut the line and stood in front of another resident who was not in the mood to tolerate his intrusion. The acrimonious verbal exchange between Bernado and the offended resident drew the attention of the staff members supervising the process. One of the staff rose from his seat at the table, went to the line, and inquired what the argument was about. He was told Bernado cut the line and was refusing to go to the back of the line and take his rightful place.

The staff told Bernado to go back to the end of the line, but he refused to comply. The staff asked Bernado to come outside with him for a short talk. Bernado did not budge. The staff then walked up to Bernado and tried to reason with him. Bernado pushed the staff, and a scuffle ensued. The second staff called out for help. I was in the small dining room, and I rushed to the scene. It took a combined effort to get Bernado under control and get him out of the large dining room. He was yelling invectives at staff as he was led to the quiet room, a place where residents under agitation were kept under supervision until they calmed down. Okor, the staff who had tried to reason with Bernado, suffered bruises to his face and hands. Sometimes such incidents further traumatize some residents with frail constitutions and suffering from emotional and psychological disorders.

"John, I heard there was a fracas in the large dining room a while ago," said Amanda.

"That is correct. You know Bernado and his stubbornness," I replied.

"What did he do this time?" asked Amanda.

"Bernado refused to wait for his turn during banking, and he cut the line. When he was asked to go back and join the line by Okor, he started a fight," I told Amanda.

"Is everybody okay?" she asked.

"Okor suffered some bruises to his face and hands, most of the residents present were okay, but Sylvia was shaken. She was visibly upset and mumbling to herself. I comforted her and took her to her room," I replied.

"What about Bernado?" Amanda asked further.

"We took him to the quiet room, and we took away his smoking privileges for the rest of the day," I told Amanda.

A few weeks after this incident, Alanzo, a handsome thirty-five-year-old resident, was admitted to Creekside. Rosalia liked him and kept him company. They were together often after program hours, watching television in the dayroom. One afternoon, residents had just finished their lunch, some were getting back to their rooms, and others were hanging out and talking to each other. Rosalia was standing in front of the residents' locker room, directly opposite nurses' station A. Bernado walked up to

Rosalia. He was never the one to speak gently. His mouth was big, and his attitude was raw.

"Your new boyfriend cannot give you satisfaction," he said to Rosalia.

"I don't know what you are talking about, Bernado," said Rosalia.

"Alanzo's penis is small. He cannot satisfy you," Bernado said to Rosalia.

"How do you know?" asked Rosalia.

"We shower in the same shower room," Bernado said.

"You are one sorry man," Rosalia told him and walked away.

I was sitting down in nurses' station A. I told Bernado his comments were inappropriate and offensive and that he should desist from it. Rosalia relayed Bernado's insult-filled comments to Alanzo. The next day at about noon, Ramon, a resident with a brown towel wrapped around his waist, stood in front of the male shower room, yelling: "There is fighting in the shower room! There is fighting in the shower room!"

I was pouring juice into cups in nurses' station A for noon medication when I heard Ramon's voice. I rushed to the male shower room. Inez followed closely behind. We found Bernado pinned to the floor by Alanzo, and we separated them. They put on their clothes, and we escorted them to the quiet room.

Bernado's comments the previous day were fresh on my mind.

"What happened, Alanzo?" I asked.

"Yesterday, Rosalia told me he made some dirty comments about me, and today he was staring at me in a funny way in the shower room, and I asked him to stop staring at me, but he did not stop. I called him a punk, and he walked up to me and hit me," Alanzo said.

"Is Alanzo's statement correct?" I asked Bernado. He did not say anything.

"Bernado, what Alanzo just said, is it true?" I asked.

Bernado refused to talk. We took his silence and lack of response as an admission of guilt, given what we knew about his belligerent character and acidic tongue.

Charge Nurse Peggy asked Alanzo to go back to his room. Bernado was asked to remain in the quiet room. I relayed to Charge Nurse Peggy the comments Bernado had made to my hearing the previous day and my admonition to him. His altercation with Alanzo was the third fistfight Bernado had been involved in. He had a brawl with his first roommate. Bernado was becoming a serious problem to the unit. Despite two transfers to two different rooms, he did not get along with his roommates. The matter was referred to the clinical director, and it was decided Bernado should be transferred to another facility. A few days after his fight with Alanzo, Bernado was taken to a maximum-security facility.

When Inez and I got into the shower room on the day of the altercation and found Bernado pinned to the floor by Alanzo, we were surprised. They were about the same height, but Bernado was more muscular. Inez said that some residents had been saying Alanzo had martial arts skill, but he did not believe it until this incident. I went to Alanzo's room to speak with him.

"I hope you did not get injured during your fight with Bernado," I said to him.

"I am fine, John," he said.

"I am curious, Alanzo. How were you able to pin Bernado to the floor? Do you watch a lot of professional wrestling?" We both laughed.

"I have martial arts skill, John. I use it for self-defense. I am not a troublemaker," he said. "I grew up in the city. Sometimes the neighborhood rascals want to prove they are tough, you have to defend yourself," he added.

I left his room, went to the nurses' station, took out his chart, and looked at it. There was no reference to any violence. I took him at his word. The rest of Alanzo's stay at Creekside was peaceful. There was no incident involving him and another resident.

Although Adolfo was one of the cool-headed residents at Creekside, unforeseen events rattled him easily. On a Thursday afternoon, he was upset because money was not available to him for canteen. Canteen was shopping time for residents inside Creekside. It was managed by the Rehabilitation Department. It was an opportunity for residents who were not able to go out on pass to get some needed provisions. Items like candy, soft drinks, and crackers were available during canteen. Money not being available to Adolfo meant he could not shop. That was bad news and a source of irritation. To let out his frustrations, he went into his room and started ripping apart his clothes. His roommate notified me of the destruction. I went to his room. He was sitting on his bed in a dejected mood, and the sadness on his face told the whole story. The damaged clothes were lying on the floor in front of him.

"Why did you rip your clothes, Adolfo?" I asked.

"There is no money for canteen. Somebody stole our canteen money," he replied. I was taken aback by Adolfo's statement. Somebody normal would be irritated at the loss of his or her property, let alone a person with emotional and psychological problems.

The previous night, during the graveyard shift, 11:00 p.m. to 7:00 a.m., a large sum of money belonging to the residents was stolen from the administrative office. Under normal circumstances, the charge nurse for that shift was the only person authorized to handle the key to the administrative office during that particular shit. It was alleged that the key to the administrative office changed hands during the graveyard shift. The circumstances as to how it happened were not clear. What was evident was that considerable amount of money belonging to the residents went missing. Pinpointing the culprit was not easy since nobody was man enough to admit he was guilty. I was disgusted when I learned of the theft. I was saying to myself, *who would stoop so low as to steal from the residents?* All they get is a mere stipend for their pocket money. The incident reminded me of a story we were told when we were growing up. A mother left her son in the custody of a next-door neighbor while she was away on an errand. She left some food with the neighbor with which to feed the lad when he got hungry. The neighbor ate the food, and the boy had no food to eat when he got hungry. A stranger came to the boy's rescue and gave him some food from his own provisions, after which he berated the boy's caretaker for his appalling conduct. The moral of the story, the storyteller told us, was that we should be true to ourselves and that we should have some principles to guide us in life. I told Adolfo management would come up with a solution to solve the problem. He calmed down and went to the dayroom to watch television.

Outing privileges were earned and approved in advance at Creekside. Outing permits were issued for the purpose of visitation to family members and friends or for shopping. High-functioning residents went out unaccompanied. Low-functioning residents ventured out with staff, family members, or friends. If a resident had been bad or disruptive, pass was denied.

Anna, Dominga's roommate, was a high-functioning resident. She had been issued a pass. Anna was born in Orange County, Southern California, but she grew up in San Francisco. She had a rough upbringing. She literarily took care of herself at an early age in a dysfunctional home, craving the acceptance she never got as a child. Anna was tall and slim, with huge eyes. She was a brunette. Anna had gone out on her pass. She left Creekside at about 2:00 p.m. Residents on pass were expected back in the facility about 6:30 p.m. At 7:00 p.m. that evening, Anna had not returned. The charge nurse on duty inquired from a staff if Anna had called to say she would be returning late. The answer was no. Nobody had heard from Anna. The charge nurse was worried about the negative response. She wondered why no one had heard from Anna. At 8:00 p.m., she decided to put in place a routine procedure for a missing person. The police were notified, they were shown Anna's picture, and told places she hung out. The search for Anna was on. For five days, Anna went missing. The police had not found her. Nobody had called Creekside to say they knew where she was. As talk of Anna's absence went on, Dominga, her roommate, said she believed Anna was somewhere in San Francisco. She said Anna loved the city. True to Dominga's statement, on the sixth day of her departure from Creekside, Anna was picked up in San Francisco and brought back to Creekside in Santa Rosa. She was slightly unkempt. Overall, she was not looking bad. She seemed guilt-ridden, knowing she had flaunted regulations. The charge nurse took her to the conference room for counseling. They were there for thirty minutes. The next day, I asked her, "Anna, why did you go AWOL (away without official leave) on your pass?"

"Oh, John, freedom is a beautiful thing. I love San Francisco. I was raised there. Here, I am reduced to regimens. I am told when to eat, when to shower, when to take my medication, when to sleep. The list goes on. San Francisco is a lively city," she continued. "Places to go and things to do. There is Chinatown, Fisherman's Wharf, the Museum of Art, the Aquarium, the Arboretum, the beach."

For a moment, which I found interesting, Anna was down-to-earth, and her real self had emerged. Her psychosis had subsided. The real woman was in front of me.

"You are here to get well, Anna. When your doctors feel you are well enough, they will let you go. Staying out of the facility longer than your pass allowed will only prolong your stay here," I said to her.

"Pray for me, John."

"I will do that," I replied.

"Thank you, John."

"You are welcome, Anna."

After she left for her room, I said to myself, *this is a young woman who would have been living a full and productive life outside Creekside if not for her mental illness.* I further said to myself, *if she would stay with her medication and not skip it like she occasionally did, she would do well in a group home for women.*

Once a year, student nurses wishing to gain some insight and experience into psychiatric nursing visit Creekside. They mingle with nurses and residents. They ask lots of questions. They were usually young, late teens and early twenties. Anna developed a bond with one of the nursing students named Paula. They spent several minutes each day discussing about things that were of interest to both of them. Paula was tall and robust, with a pretty face and big bosom. She told Anna she was born in Pennsylvania but her parents moved to San Francisco where she grew up. Both women knew San Francisco very well, and that was what brought them together.

Anna saw in Paula a woman in her full bloom enjoying her youth, going about her affairs and making good and worthy preparations for the rest of her life. This was what Anna would have wanted for herself, if not for her mental illness. Paula was living a life Anna would have cherished, if not for her confinement to a mental institution.

The interesting observation I made about the presence of the student nurses was that the residents tended to behave themselves better when the students were around. Consequently, the students did not gain much or had no good insight into how stressful psychiatric nursing can sometimes be at the end of their stay.

Anna and Paula's conversations were mostly about movies and boyfriends. Paula had an engagement ring on her finger. She planned to marry her fiancé after the completion of her program. He was a computer technician working with a software company in San Francisco. Paula spoke kindly and respectfully about her fiancée to Anna.

The student nurses' sojourn was about two weeks duration, during which they tailed nurses and psychiatric technicians, and they asked questions about medications and some of the teachings they received in the classroom and how it related to the real world of psychiatric nursing. After they were gone, things went back as they were. Some residents who seemed to have gone into hibernation, so to speak, resumed their naughty behavior at full throttle.

Mental health hospitals as depicted in movies were largely located on the outskirts of town. Creekside was real and was located inside Santa Rosa, along Sonoma Avenue. There was nothing assuming about Creekside. On the outside, it looked like a normal property in a regular neighborhood. It shared the same vicinity with a nursing home for the elderly. On the inside though, especially on heated days, when some residents go haywire, it was a different story. It was not uncommon for two or three residents to be erratic at about the same time and throw the whole unit into turmoil. Two residents could be having heated verbal exchanges which could lead to a fistfight unless quelled down and brought under control by staff. Another resident, out of sheer panic or heightened psychosis, went berserk and became a nuisance to his roommates or other residents. Incidents such as these were more rampant during the afternoon shifts. During the morning shifts, residents were usually sedated, and a serene atmosphere pervaded the facility.

On their return from pass, residents were supposed to be thoroughly searched for contrabands. These ranged from illegal drugs, such as marijuana or crack cocaine, to any object that could inflict injury on anybody, such as a knife. Somehow, Bud, a resident, was able to sneak some boxes of matches into the facility, unbeknownst to the mental health worker who searched him after his return from pass. Bud was once a promising student at an Ivy League institution. He suffered a breakdown during an examination week, and he never recovered. He hallucinated and was emotionally unstable. Keeping to himself most of the time and when he stepped out, he had the tendency to circle the same spot for minutes. Sometimes he stood at a sport and stared into space for quite a while. Outdoor breaks where smoking was allowed were the only time you saw him near other residents. Even then, his response to attempts from his peers to get him to talk to them was reduced to monosyllables.

During an outdoor break I was supervising, Bud secretly lit his cigarette. At the start of outdoor break, a number of residents surrounded the mental health worker supervising the break, wanting their cigarettes lit. I did not see Bud lighting up his own cigarette. Fortunately, Pete's watchful eyes caught him lighting his cigarette. Under Creekside regulation, it was the staff supervising the break who provided lighter or matches for residents. For safety reasons, residents were not allowed to keep any form of incendiary material in their possession. Pete came to me and said, "John, Bud lit his own cigarette with matches."

"Are you sure?" I asked Pete.

"Yes, John, I saw him."

I approached Bud and I asked him, "Bud, did you light up your cigarette yourself?"

Bud kept quiet. He did not answer my question. I turned to two residents standing near him, and I asked them if any of them had lit Bud's cigarette with their own cigarette. They both said no.

"Don't burn down this building, Bud. Give up the matches. We all have to have a roof over our heads," said Pete.

"I do not think Pete is lying. Give me the matches, Bud," I said to him.

He did not budge. "I am going to search you," I said.

He then reached into the right pocket of his pants and brought out a box of matches. I took it from him.

"Thank you," I said to him.

Bud then walked up to where Pete was standing and got in his face.

"Are you now the policeman at Creekside, you piece of shit," Bud said to Pete.

"Break it up, guys. There will be consequences for fighting," I said to them. They heeded my warning and dispersed.

When the outdoor break was over, I reported the matter to Charge Nurse Peggy. She called Bud to the quiet room and asked me to go search his room. After a thorough search, I found two boxes of matches hidden among his clothes in his drawer. Charge Nurse Peggy showed the two boxes of matches to Bud, and he owned up. He did not deny he had matches in his drawer. She warned Bud about contravening the rules and regulations of the facility. She told him there would be severe repercussions the next time matches or any other contraband was found in his possession. An impromptu meeting of mental health workers was convened. Charge Nurse Peggy urged us to do a better job of searching the residents on their return from pass. She reminded us that we were dealing with mentally and emotionally unstable people and that an outbreak of fire at Creekside would be catastrophic for both residents and staff. I shared the concerns of Charge Nurse Peggy. Proper performance of our duties was something we owed to the residents. We had jobs at Creekside because the residents were there.

Most of the residents at Creekside were in their twenties or thirties. A few were in their forties. These were people with mental health issues or addiction problems. A milestone was reached at Creekside when on a bright and sunny day in June, an eighteen-year-old youngster, a male named Musa, was admitted to the center. Musa was autistic and claustrophobic. He was solitary and noninteractive with people. He had one thing going for him though. He had a loving and caring family. Musa was of average height, dark hair, a bright face, and an engaging smile. He was a low-functioning resident. He needed lots of help with his activities of daily living. After admission formalities, I took him to his room. His roommate Adolfo was not there.

"Musa, I will be back to take you on a tour of the facility," I said to him.

"Okay," he said.

After about twenty-five minutes, I went back to his room. The door was ajar. Musa was lying down on his bed.

"Are you ready, Musa?" I asked.

"Yes, I am," he said.

"Let's go," I said.

He rose from his bed and walked out of his room. We walked to the dayroom.

"This is the dayroom. After program hours, you can watch television here and socialize with other residents," I said to him.

His roommate Adolfo was in the dayroom. I introduced them.

"Adolfo, this is Musa, your new roommate."

"What kind of name is that?" asked Adolfo.

"It is a Muslim name. My parents came from the Middle East. I was born here in America." said Musa.

"I am a Christian," Adolfo said to him.

Musa's next statement made my day. I never expected such a mature response from an eighteen-year-old kid.

"Whether Christian or Muslim, it is one God," said Musa.

Adolfo shook hands with Musa and said to him, "It is nice to meet you."

Our tour continued. We moved to the laundry room.

"This is where you wash your dirty clothes." I handed him a leaflet containing the days and time he can do his laundry. "We provide the soap," I added. Our next stop was the male shower room.

"This is the male shower room. You have to take your shower before 9:00 p.m. No resident is allowed in the shower room after that time."

"Why is that?" asked Musa.

"It is the facility's regulation. There are rules and regulations residents have to obey while staying at Creekside," I said.

We moved to the large dining room. Musa was on a regular diet. "This is the large dining room. Residents on a regular diet eat here. This is where you will be having your meals," I told him.

It was almost dinnertime. Residents were already gathering in the large dining room for their meal. I ushered Musa in. He sat down and waited along with the other residents. Food was served, and Musa was shy to eat in the presence of so many unfamiliar faces. He sat down speechless and gazed at his meal. Adolfo, always with a voracious appetite, had finished his food and came to me and said, "John, Musa is sitting down in the dining room, but he is not eating. His tray is in front of him."

"Did anything go wrong, Adolfo?" I asked him.

"You mean in the dining room?"

"Yes," I said.

"Nothing happened, nothing that I know of," Adolfo said.

I went to the large dining room to talk to Musa. When I got there, he had already given out his tray.

"Where is your food?" I asked him.

"I gave it away," he said.

"Why?"

"I am not hungry," he replied.

I had the feeling he was not telling me the truth. I probed further.

"What is going on, Musa?" I asked him.

"I am shy. These faces are all unfamiliar to me," he said.

"You will get over it. These faces were once new like yours. If you get hungry, let me know. I will find something for you to eat," I told him.

Unlike Musa who was calm and shy, Rosalia was a study in contrast. On her good days, she was warm and friendly. On her bad days, you wouldn't want to be anywhere near her and would avoid her like the plague. Rosalia was tall and slender. She had an oval face and eyes that turned gunmetal under agitation. She had a rough childhood in a rough neighborhood. Born out of wedlock, she did not know her father. She moved periodically with her troubled mother, living for some time with her grandparents. Her instability was such that she did not complete her education. She dropped out of school. Her life thereafter went downhill. She got involved with drugs and was indiscriminate in her dealings with boys. She slept with any male who was willing to spend some money on her. She got arrested for drugs at age fifteen and for public drunkenness and disorderly conduct a year later. Being a minor, she had to go through the juvenile system. At seventeen, she was arraigned for prostitution and handled as an adult, although she had not attained the legal age of eighteen. Her record did not paint a pretty picture but was filthy from the perspective of the authorities. They decided it was high time she was handled appropriately. Rosalia was taken to a home for troubled women where the intervention of a social worker proved decisive. After counseling, she agreed to get off the street and straighten out her life. She spoke about her desire to go back to school and complete her education and thereafter get a job to support herself. This was a lofty goal Rosalia could attain if she was stable, reliable, and free from street drugs. Something had to be done to address these issues. She also suffered from an eating disorder. She needed the attention of a specialist. It was at this juncture the authorities referred her to Creekside.

Rosalia was fond of jewelry, cheap gold rings and necklaces. She was once taken to the emergency room because the ring she had on her finger was so tight it was hurting her. Neither she nor any staff member could pull out the ring despite the application of lubricants to her finger. The ring was dislodged at the emergency room of a local hospital. As a result, she was discouraged from wearing jewelry. Rosalia was adamant and insisted on continuing the practice. On a Wednesday afternoon, Rosalia was seen with some jewelry, which was promptly taken away from her. She got agitated and started yelling invectives at the staff who took the jewelry away from her. Charge Nurse Peggy requested that she be taken to the quiet room, and she left for her lunch break. Rosalia was given some medication to help her calm down. The psychiatric technician who gave her the medication wanted Rosalia to spend some time in the quiet room. Before the medication given to her could take effect, the assistant director of nursing, who was temporarily acting as charge nurse while Charge Nurse Peggy was on her lunch break, released Rosalia from the quiet room and gave her back her jewelry. On her way to her room, Rosalia threw her jewelry at Amanda and snarled at her, "You bitch, get out of my way." Rosalia got into her room and started yelling at the top of her voice, upsetting her roommates. Inez and I went to her room to try to talk to her and see if we could calm her down.

"Rosalia, you are disturbing your roommates. Stop the yelling, calm down," Inez said to her. She did not listen. She continued shouting and letting out abusive words at Inez and me.

"Let's take her back to the quiet room. She will be by herself there. She will not be a nuisance to her roommates," I said to Inez.

"The assistant director of nursing asked her to go back to her room," Inez replied.

We both left the room. A few minutes later, Rosalia escalated. She ripped apart the sheets on her bed and threw them out the window. She destroyed other items in her room. One of her roommates rushed to the nursing station and alerted us. Inez, Amanda, and I rushed to their room. Inez led the way. As soon as Inez stepped into their room, Rosalia jumped on him and started swinging at Inez with both of her hands. Inez defended himself by raising his hands and shielding his face from the punches Rosalia was throwing at him. It was like a boxing tournament between two unevenly matched contestants. Amanda and I took hold of Rosalia's hands and separated her from Inez. She was taken away to the seclusion room in walking restraints and put on four-point restraints on a bed. The seclusion room was where residents who have reacted violently to a staff or fellow resident were kept for a while for them to cool off and calm down. The psychiatric technician who had earlier given medication to Rosalia and had wanted her to spend some time in the quiet room frowned when he learned she was allowed back to her room before the medication given to her could kick in.

"Who let Rosalia back to her room?" he asked.

"The assistant director of nursing sent her back to her room," Inez replied.

"Inez, was this a case of miscommunication, or am I getting something wrong here?" the psychiatric technician asked.

"I don't know, Bob, I really don't know," Inez said to him.

Bob shook his head and walked away. Inez turned to me and started blaming me for not doing enough to stop Rosalia from hitting him.

"Inez, if you had listened to my suggestion to take Rosalia back to the quiet room, this incident would not have happened," I said to him.

"In hindsight, John, you were right," he said.

Inez was not a new staff. He was aware of Rosalia's truculent nature under agitation. Taking her back to the quiet room, where she would cool off, was the best course of action under the circumstances.

The next day, Rosalia was sitting at a table in the small dining room. The small dining room was for diabetics and residents with eating disorders. Rosalia had an eating disorder, so she ate in the small dining room. I was out of the small dining room for a few minutes to use the restroom. On my return, I discovered there was a heated verbal exchange between Amanda and Rosalia. Rosalia had swapped her food tray with another resident. That was against the rules. Residents who ate in the small dining room were not allowed to exchange their food so as not to defeat the purpose of the exercise. Rosalia was asked by Amanda to return the food tray with her and take back what came from the kitchen for her. She refused. I wanted the two women to settle their differences, thinking Amanda could handle the situation. Their argument became a shouting match.

"Give back the food tray, Rosalia," Amanda said.

"Leave me alone. I will not give back the food tray," Rosalia replied.

"Oh, you think you are tough, Rosalia," said Amanda.

"I am tough," Rosalia replied.

As Amanda walked toward Rosalia to ask her to surrender the food tray she was holding, Rosalia quickly placed the food tray she had with her on the table in front of her. She grabbed the cup of water on the tray, threw it at Amanda, and hit her. Amanda, knowing fully well whom she was facing, and knowing that Rosalia was a damn good boxer, speedily grabbed Rosalia's hands. Before the situation could deteriorate further, I intervened by placing myself between the two women.

"Have you forgotten what happened yesterday?" I said to Rosalia.

"No," she replied.

"Make it easy on yourself. You are following me to the quiet room," I said.

I led the way, and she followed me. In the quiet room, Charge Nurse Peggy took over. She talked to Rosalia on the need to abide by regulations and keep to her diet plan. After twenty minutes, Rosalia came back to the small dining room.

"Could you say 'I am sorry' to Amanda?" I said to her.

She looked at me, then turned and stared at Amanda for some seconds.

"I am sorry, Amanda," she said.

She then sat down and ate the food that came from the kitchen for her.

Every Friday, Rosalia presented the sunny side of her personality. Every Friday evening, there was excitement and electricity at Creekside. Friday evening was social gathering day. For 120 minutes, there was entertainment, soft drinks, fruits, and sandwiches, along with music. It started at about 8:00 p.m. and ended around 10:00 p.m. Rosalia loved music. She loved to sing and dance. She moved with the grace and agility of an accomplished dancer. I was always amazed at the different personality she presented every Friday evening during social gathering time. "I Got You Babe" by Sonny and Cher was one of her favorite songs. She sang along with karaoke music, swaying from side to side. The karaoke music was followed by disco songs. Rosalia took to the floor as if to say "I will show you what I have got." She danced toward a male resident and picked him for her dancing partner. Other residents joined in. The large dining room came alive with the sound of music, dancing, and laughter. Even residents sitting on chairs were laughing and giggling, talking animatedly among themselves. A big contrast to some of the scenes of aloofness and taciturn we witnessed earlier in the week. I saw the two hours of socializing as therapeutic. Residents who were usually melancholic and sometimes belligerent were in bright moods. Music had a soothing effect, if only for a short while, on some residents.

Creekside mental health center was fenced. The only entrance and exit from the facility was an electronic door controlled at the nurses' station. At the initial stage of his stay at Creekside, Musa stayed a lot in his room. Being claustrophobic, he found Creekside confining. Instead of making a dramatic escape by scaling over the fence, which he could not do since he was not a good high jumper, Musa chose a less dramatic route. He chose to sneak around the electronic door and made his escape when a visitor was buzzed in or out and the staff at the nurses' station was not paying attention. Often, it was a staff on break at the patio or a resident sitting or standing by the fence who noticed his flight and raised the alarm by rushing to the nurses' desk. Musa was not a good high jumper, but he was a good runner. After three grueling chases to get Musa back to the facility, the clinical director came up with a new initiative. Musa was to be taken on walks with staff several times a week. That was a game changer. Musa did not run away from Creekside after the new policy was implemented.

Adolfo, Musa's roommate, came to me one morning and said, "John, Musa is one funny guy."

"What do you mean?" I asked.

"Musa showers with his clothes on. I have never seen anybody showering with their clothes on," said Adolfo.

I pondered Adolfo's statement for some minutes and said, "I will talk to him." That same day, Pete approached me and said the same thing.

"Is something wrong with Muss's penis and he is afraid we will make fun of him and tell the girls? He showers with his clothes on," said Pete.

Pete, always the funny one, changed Musa to Muss.

"Adolfo told me the same thing earlier," I said to Pete.

When I took Musa for his walk, we went to the mall and window-shopped. Musa liked Chinese food. We bought Chinese food, sat down, and ate.

"Musa, why do you shower with your clothes on?" I asked him.

"I am shy," he said.

"It is a male shower room. No female is coming in there," I said to him. "You cannot have a clean and thorough bath with your clothes on. It is important you rinse your body thoroughly when you shower," I added.

We finished eating and walked back to the facility. On his way to his room, I reminded him of his shower and the proper way to go about it. The next two days, I did the same thing. A week later, Musa reported to me that he no longer showers with his clothes on and that it feels good. "That is the right way to go, Musa. Keep up the good work," I said to him. To my joy and satisfaction, both Adolfo and

Pete confirmed Musa's statement. I felt it was small but significant progress.

After leaving the dining room one afternoon, Musa started complaining of pain inside his jaw. The next day, he had a swollen cheek. He had difficulty chewing and swallowing solid food. He had to go on a soft diet like Jell-O and yogurt for the time being. I teased him that he was now a toothless old man. His tooth was the problem. Musa had to go to town to see the doctor, and arrangements were made. I had to accompany him downtown to see the dentist. If this problem had cropped up shortly after his admission to Creekside, there would have been apprehension Musa might bolt. Fortunately, the clinical director had already put in place a routine whereby staff had to take Musa out several times weekly outside the center. The worry he might split during his visit to the dentist was at a minimum.

The doctor was a middle-aged man, clean-shaven, with a spotless lab coat. He introduced himself.

"Is it going to hurt, Doc?" asked Musa.

"Let's see what is going on in your mouth and where we go from there," said the dentist.

Musa laid down on the examination bed and opened his mouth. The doctor looked inside his mouth for a few minutes. "Abscess," he declared. "It could be taken care of with antibiotics. Try antibiotics for two weeks, and if the pain doesn't go away,

I will pull the tooth that is hurting," he added. Being a layman, I thought the doctor's approach was reasonable. Musa was dreadful about going to the dentist. He summoned the courage to go, and his immediate worry about his tooth removal was allayed. He took his antibiotics for two weeks. I saw to it that he washed his mouth daily with mouthwash and that he brushed his teeth. This combination worked. Musa's tooth pain was gone. There was no need to go back to the dentist. My own personal experience came into play. It served as a useful lesson. Some years ago, I was experiencing some pain in my mouth. My tooth was hurting me. A friend told me specifically to use Listerine mouthwash daily and brush my teeth with Colgate toothpaste. Before the onset of my pain, I rarely used mouthwash, and I bought any toothpaste I came across first at the supermarket. My friend's advice turned out to be just what the doctor ordered. My tooth pain went away. That was why I recommended the same thing for Musa, and it worked.

Musa's mother and senior brother, Abdul, came to visit him once a month. For Musa, his family visit was always a big day. I ensured that he showered and that he was neat and tidy. The same thing applied to his room. On such days, Musa's face seemed to brighten more, anticipating the goodies from his mother. His mother and brother usually arrived around 2:00 p.m., bearing Chinese food, candies, soft drinks, and clean clothes for him. While Musa and his brother ate, his mother engaged me in conversation.

"John, how is he doing?" his mother asked.

"He is improving gradually," I replied. "He no longer showers with his clothes on, with my help he is keeping his room tidy, and he interacts a bit with other residents," I added.

"I am glad to hear that," his mother said.

She left for the nurses' station to talk to the charge nurse. I waited for Musa and his brother to finish eating, and I joined them. Abdul was a soccer enthusiast, and we talked about soccer.

"Soccer is the dominant sports in other parts of the world. It was invented by the British and exported to their colonies. In this modern day, soccer competition between former colonial masters and their former colonies give World Cup matches much excitement," I said.

"Why is soccer not popular in America?" asked Abdul.

"It is picking up, but American football and baseball have more fans. Sometimes soccer ends in a draw. Americans don't like sports that end in a draw. They want to see a winner. That, I think, is one reason soccer is not very popular in America," I said. "In Africa where I was born, soccer is a passion. Kids as young as seven or eight years old turn rags into balls and flattish spaces into playing fields. They play barefooted. Their goal is happiness. They kick and chase handmade balls with skill and pleasure. A few lucky ones amongst these kids grow up with remarkable skills, good moves, and beautiful control of football on the playing field. These lucky ones are picked up, and they play for the national teams. Some are even recruited by European clubs and are taken abroad where they dazzle large crowds of soccer enthusiasts with their skills far away from the villages and small towns where they were born," I added.

"I like soccer. My friends and I play all the time in the summer. When the weather gets bad, we play indoor soccer," said Abdul.

"Friendship is a good thing. It is the idea behind World Cup soccer and the Olympic games. The two sporting events are designed to foster friendship and goodwill amongst various countries of the world," I said.

"John, I have watched the Olympic games on television. How did it get started?" asked Musa.

"The Olympic games began many, many years ago at Mount Olympus, in Greece. Then, it was just the Greeks who competed amongst themselves every four years. Later, other countries of the world joined in. The venue for the Olympic games alternates every four years to a different country, depending on the country that won the right to host the next game. There are winter and summer Olympic games. The last summer Olympic games in America was in Atlanta in 1996," I said.

"John, what country is the best in soccer?" asked Abdul.

"There are many countries good at soccer. Brazil, Italy, Spain, France, Germany, and Argentina are amongst some of them."

"World Cup in soccer and the Olympic games, which is more popular?" Abdul followed up.

"Both games are very popular. They draw a very large crowd of enthusiastic fans all around the world every four years. As regards soccer, it is almost a religion in some countries with devotees. It is not uncommon in such places for fans to wake up at 3:00 a.m. during World Cup matches to watch and root for their teams. For such ardent fans, they argue World Cup soccer is more popular than the Olympic games," I said. "For such enthusiastic soccer fans, it was always a joy for them to be a part of the many millions of people around the world watching over thirty nations abide by the rules that govern the sport," I added.

"John, is it clubs or national teams that provide the players for the World Cup competition?" asked Abdul.

"It is the national team, but they are made up of players from various clubs in the respective countries. In places like Brazil and Italy, these clubs are owned by fabulously rich business people who spend enormous amounts of money to attract top players to their clubs," I said.

"So the soccer players are rich?" Abdul further asked.

"Some of them are very rich. Aside from the money they make in soccer, the best players have advertisement contracts with some of the most popular sports garment and shoe manufacturers of the world," I said to them.

"So sports is big business?" Abdul continued.

"You are right, Abdul. Sports is a multibillion-dollar business in the industrialized world. You have an inquiring mind, Abdul. That is good for you," I said.

Musa's mother concluded her talk with the charge nurse and joined us. It was time for her and his brother to take their leave. They gave him hugs and told him they will see him next month.

Musa and Adolfo got along well as roommates. It turned out they both had something in common; they liked Chinese food, funny movies, and comedies. On a warm summer afternoon in August, Adolfo's uncle Ernesto, visited him and took both Adolfo and Musa for an outing. Passes for both of them had been arranged in advance. Some days earlier, Adolfo had asked if he and Musa could go out together, adding that his uncle would take them out. Charge Nurse Peggy was delighted to approve their passes. She was always encouraged by residents who shared the same room and got along well; harmony was her forte.

As Ernesto, Adolfo, and Musa were stepping out, Pete said to them, "On your way back, guys, sneak in some beer, and we will have a wild party with the girls after lights out. Hahahaha." He laughed. "Just kidding, guys, just kidding," he added.

"Who is more clownish, Adolfo, you or Pete?" asked Musa. Ernesto, Adolfo, Musa, Pete, and myself all cracked up.

After lunch at a local Chinese restaurant, they went to watch a movie at one of the cinema houses in town. They returned to the facility in the evening.

"How was the outing, guys?" I asked them.

"It was great," said Adolfo. "We had Chinese food for lunch, and we went to see *My Big Fat Greek Weeding*, a very funny movie," he explained.

They both started laughing. I sensed they must have had a good time.

"Was the movie actually about a wedding?" I asked.

"Yes. Like the title suggested, it was about a wedding, but at first, the father of the bride was reluctant to accept the guy his daughter was about to marry. He complained he did not know whether the guy was good or bad," said Adolfo.

"It is a typical stance of some parents when their daughter is about to marry. They worry she may have fallen for the wrong guy," I said.

"He was funny though," said Musa.

"What scenes did you find funny, Musa?" I asked.

"The father of the bride believed that Windex could cure minor ailments. He applied Windex to boil and also to skin rash," Musa said. "There was also a scene where the bridegroom bumped into a stranger in the street because he was not paying attention to where he was going. The woman he bumped into reacted angrily by hitting him with her handbag."

"Wow," I uttered.

"What scene did you find funny, Adolfo?" I asked.

"There was this scene where the bridegroom was tricked by his brothers-in-law to tell the assembled family in Greek that he has three testicles. Every normal man has two testicles, not three. The bridegroom found out he had been fooled by the astonished look the family members gave him. He was embarrassed. His brothers-in-law who pulled the trick on him ran away. He pursued them."

"That is very funny," I said.

"What kind of movie do you like, John?" asked Adolfo.

"I like Westerns, I like war movies, and I like funny movies like you guys do. When it comes to Western movies, John Wayne was my hero. He was very good. John Wayne was also good in his non-Western movies. He was one of the actors in *The Longest Day*, a war movie. It was a good one," I said.

"My father likes war movies too. My grandpa was a marine during the Second World War. What other war movie have you seen?" asked Adolfo.

"I have seen *Saving Private Ryan*. Tom Hanks was the lead actor. It was about finding and bringing back home Private Ryan, whose brothers, three of them, had been killed in the same war. It would have been too much for one family to bear if all four brothers had died in the same war. It was very emotional. Tom Hanks did an excellent job. The movie won five Academy Awards," I said.

"Going back to John Wayne, I have heard of John Wayne Airport in Orange County, Southern California. Was the airport named after the actor?" asked Adolfo.

"Yes, the airport was named after John Wayne. He was living not far from the airport. The airport was formerly known as Orange County Airport. After John Wayne's death, the airport was renamed in his memory," I said.

"What funny movie have you seen lately, John?" asked Musa.

"Not lately, but I remember a very hilarious movie I saw in the past, *Back to School* by Rodney Dangerfield. It was a comedy in a class by itself. It was very funny," I said.

"Is Rodney Dangerfield still living?" asked Adolfo.

"It really does not matter whether a good entertainer is dead or alive. One of the fine points about good entertainers is that long after they are gone, their memories live on in what they left behind. Generations yet unborn will enjoy their work. Fortunately for America, there are good entertainers in this country," I said.

"We enjoyed our outing, John," said Adolfo.

"I am happy for both of you. It seems you had a good time. Enjoy the rest of the evening," I said to them.

As time progressed, things turned around for the better for Musa. He took his showers every day. The same thing applied to his oral care, and to an appreciable degree, his room was tidy. These were small but significant steps. It pointed to some degree of normalcy. It was some of the things normal people did every day. Looking back at when he first arrived at Creekside, Musa had made some progress. I lent a helping hand when I saw things that needed to be straightened out in his room, such as putting dirty clothes in the laundry basket or hanging up clothes that were not immediately needed for use in the wardrobe.

The one area Musa was lagging behind was better interaction with other residents. The thinking at Creekside was, Musa, being a gentle character and not a troublemaker, would do well in a group home for boys. The next step in his rehabilitation was getting him out of his isolationist tendency. Pete and Adolfo were enlisted in the bid to get Musa more involved with his peers. They enticed him to a weekend of outing if he played cards and basketball with them on weekdays. Chinese food would be included in the outing, courtesy of Charge Nurse Peggy. Musa took up the offer. The prospect of a Saturday or Sunday outing with the possibility of Chinese food thrown in was too alluring to bypass. When they were not playing cards or basketball, Pete and Adolfo engaged Musa in conversations about movies and baseball. Although Pete and Adolfo did most of the talking, Musa listened and asked some questions. This went on for eight weeks. It became a routine. Musa looked forward to his cards and basketball games weekdays and to his outing on Saturday or Sunday.

After twelve weeks of uninterrupted progress, Charge Nurse Peggy decided Musa was ready for a group home. A search for a place where he would fit in commenced. After three weeks of intensive search, a group home for boys some miles away from Santa Rosa was located. Charge Nurse Peggy informed Musa that he would be moving in a few days.

"Back home?" came his question.

"No, to a group home. You will be there with boys about your age," said Charge Nurse Peggy.

One could sense the feeling of apprehension of the unknown in Musa.

"How is it different from here?" came his next question.

"You have more freedom of movement," said Charge Nurse Peggy.

"You might have to take more responsibility for your activities of daily living such as cleaning your own room or doing your own laundry," she added.

"Can my mother and brother come visit me?" he asked.

"Yes, they will be able to visit you," said Charge Nurse Peggy.

"John, will you come visit me?" Musa asked.

"When you get there, Musa, make us happy by being a good resident and obey the rules, and I will come visit you," I said.

A week later, there was a small send-off party for Musa. He was the first autistic resident Creekside had handled, and it seemed Creekside did not botch the job. His mother and brother were there for the send-off party. There were hugs, wishes, and feelings of goodwill. Musa left for his new abode in the company of his mother and brother and an official from the group home.

May 2001, Chico, a wheelchair-bound resident with cerebral palsy, was admitted to Creekside. He had lots of challenges. Chico could not walk on his own. He had to be helped. He could not take his shower by himself. He needed assistance. Even using the restroom, he had to be wheeled in and assisted onto the commode. The picture was clear. He was a very dependent resident. He needed lots of help with his activities of daily living. In May when Chico came into Creekside, the two beds in room 409 were occupied. I was responsible for the two residents in the room. Room 407 had an empty bed but was assigned to another mental health worker. To ensure caregiving for Chico was entrusted to me, Ramon, one of the residents in room 409, was asked to move to room 407.

"John, I really don't want to move," said Ramon. "I like this room, and when I move out, it means I will no longer have you as my mental health worker, and I really don't want that," he added.

"Take it easy, Ramon. Do what the charge nurse has asked you to do. If you need help with something, let me know, and I will see what I can do to assist you," I said.

The exchange of rooms was implemented. Ramon moved to room 407, and Chico took his old bed in room 409. Chico took his shower every other day. I helped him with it. Part of Chico's daily therapy included assisting him with his walking exercise, which I conducted with the help of a four-legged walker. I followed Chico closely behind with his wheelchair, steadied him when he lost his balance, and I asked him to sit down in his wheelchair when I perceived he was tired. We did this twice a day. It was a chore that needed lots of patience, but then that was what we were there for in the first place.

Chico's last shower was on a Saturday. He was due for another shower on a Monday, but I was off duty that Monday. When I came back to work on Tuesday, it was documented on the activities of daily living chart that Chico had a shower on Monday.

"Would you help me with a shower, John?" Chico said to me.

"It is documented in the chart that you had a shower yesterday," I said to him.

"Nobody helped me with a shower yesterday," he said.

I went and talked to Inez, whose signature was on the chart.

"Inez, you documented on the activities of daily living chart that Chico had a shower yesterday, and he is telling me that was not the case," I said to him.

"I am busy, John. I don't have time to talk," Inez said to me.

Inez was in a room, making a resident's bed. I went back to Chico.

"It is Inez's signature on the chart, and he does not want to talk," I said.

"I will talk to Charge Nurse Peggy, and I will like you to be there, John," Chico said to me.

I helped him into his wheelchair and wheeled him to the nurses' station. "Charge Nurse Peggy, John told me Inez wrote down I took a shower yesterday, and I did not," Chico said to her.

Charge Nurse Peggy took a look at the activity of daily living chart and found my statement to be true.

"John, tell Inez I want to see him," said Charge Nurse Peggy.

I left for the room where I had seen him earlier. He had finished making the bed, and he had gone into the dayroom. I told him the charge nurse wanted to see him. He frowned. After some minutes of hesitation, he followed me to the nurses' station. Charge Nurse Peggy had the activities of daily living chart in front of her.

"This is your signature, Inez, is it not?"

"Um, um, um, it is. I must have made some mistake," he said.

"John was off yesterday, and Chico was assigned to you. Is that correct?" she asked.

"That is correct," Inez said.

"If Chico was assigned to you yesterday, how can your signature here be an error?" Inez was silent. "This is falsification, Inez. Elsewhere, it could land you in hot water," said Charge Nurse Peggy, looking very irritated. "This is the last time this happens. If it happens again, I am taking the matter to the clinical director, and you know what that means," Charge Nurse Peggy admonished. "Now take Chico to the shower room and help him with his shower," Charge Nurse Peggy told Inez.

"I am doing some laundry for residents," put in Inez.

"I will help Chico with his shower," I said to the charge nurse.

"Thank you, John. I know I can count on you," said Charge Nurse Peggy.

Inez was a puzzling character. Before Creekside, he had led a double life in Oakland, a city not far from San Francisco. His job as a nurse assistant in a local nursing home was a cover for his gang-ster affiliation. A galling story he told me about his encounter with a gang sent cold shivers down my spine. He was jumped on his way back home from work. A gang surrounded him and had him down in a second. They had his arms and legs pinned down. One of them sat on his chest. Inez was suffocat-ing. He was slugged repeatedly. There was nothing one man could do against such an overwhelming force. He swore at his tormentors between gasps. Inez's swearing brought on more punishment. When he realized they could hurt him badly, he started screaming wildly. One of the gang members tried to silence him by placing a hand over his mouth. Inez bit the intruding hand so badly it bled to the extent that Inez had some blood in his mouth. The injury elicited a wild scream from the injured gang member. The scream was so piercing it attracted the attention of people in the neighborhood. That was Inez's saving grace. The gang fled from the scene. Inez's life was spared, but serious damage had been done to him. He was badly bruised. He was smarting and aching, and his whole body was sore for days. He was scared of his own shadow after the beating he received from the gang. When he recovered, he never walked alone, and he always carried a knife for protection. He decided belonging to a rival gang served his immediate need which was how best to survive in a very rough neighborhood.

After he joined a rival gang, the neighborhood hotheads left him alone for a while. They stopped messing with him. As weeks turned into months, the situation worsened for Inez. When the going got really tough and he feared for his life, Inez absconded from Oakland and sought refuge in Santa Rosa, a small town removed from the hustle and bustle of city life. Inez said he was a changed man, but his actions told a different story. Wild tales of his gangster days made the hair on the back of your neck stand up. Inez was short and stout. He wore his hair short. He had an oval-shaped face that sometimes wore a cynical smile. He had the swagger and brashness of someone used to giving commands, although those commands were in the underworld of gangster land. Some of the cruelties he depicted in his stories were chilling. I asked him how someone becomes so insensitive and punitive. "Years of living in the street taught gangs how to shut off their feelings and emotions. They become hardened by the callousness and brutality they see every day in the street," he said. I further asked him what it was like belonging to a gang. "It was rough, John. You see a lot, not the right things though. You also learn a lot, but much of what you learn is useless for life in the real world," he said.

Charge Nurse Peggy sometimes considered Pete a pain in the butt. She found some of Pete's antics annoying, even bordering on selfishness and pettiness. In a meeting, Pete demanded to know why residents' cigarettes were locked up in lockers opposite nursing station A. The charge nurse kept the key. Previously, residents were allowed to keep their own cigarettes.

"Could you explain to me, Pete, how come all of a sudden, Ramon smokes two packs of cigarettes a day?" asked Charge Nurse Peggy. "Ramon is not a heavy smoker. It is either he is giving it away or somebody is stealing it from him. I have asked him about it, and he has refused to talk. He said to me he does not want to talk about it. It seems somebody has bullied him into keeping his mouth shut," she added.

"If Ramon decides to be generous with his cigarettes, it is his own business," said Pete.

"The fact that he refuses to talk about it tells me he is not giving them out of his own free will. Somebody is coercing him into giving them out," said Charge Nurse Peggy.

"I don't think that is the case, Peggy," said Pete.

"As far as I am concerned, the matter is settled, Pete. Residents' cigarettes will remain locked up in the lockers," Charge Nurse Peggy maintained.

"What about during outing, can residents leave with their cigarettes?" asked Pete.

"That policy has changed too. High-functioning residents will be allowed to go out with their cigarettes. For low-functioning residents, even during outing, staff will supervise their smoking," Charge Nurse Peggy said.

"Why these changes all of a sudden?" asked Pete.

"I don't care how many cigarettes you smoke, Pete. Just provide your own cigarettes and don't pester other residents for cigarettes," Charge Nurse Peggy told him.

"Now the truth comes out. You think, Peggy, I am pestering residents for cigarettes. I will make a deal with you. I will buy my own cigarettes, show them to you, and keep them myself. How about that?" said Pete.

"The rules remain as it is. Pete, while you are in the facility, cigarettes will be kept in the resident lockers. There is no going around the rules," said Charge Nurse Peggy.

"You are one bad cop, Peggy. Hahahaha." Pete laughed.

After this exchange, Charge Nurse Peggy called me to the nurses' station. The issue about smoking and Pete's demands was a trifle but annoying to Charge Nurse Peggy. To Pete though, it was a big deal.

"I am of the opinion, John, that Pete is a manipulator. He wants the rules about cigarettes changed, and I am not going to relax the rules to suit him. I have made it clear to him that the rules remain the same, and he still wants to argue with me," said Peggy.

"It is nicotine addiction, Peggy. He is addicted to nicotine. The craving is strong. I do not think his intention is to give you a hard time," I said.

"You think so, John?" she asked.

"I think so, Peggy," I said.

"Would you talk to him and impress upon him that it is imperative that rules are adhered to?" said Peggy. "It will also be good if you can urge him to cut down on the number of cigarettes he smokes a day for his own good," Peggy said with a smile.

She knew that was a daunting task, talking to Pete about cutting down on the number of cigarettes he smoked per day. I did not go to Pete immediately after discussing the matter with Charge Nurse Peggy. He would know that it was Charge Nurse Peggy who asked me to talk to him. I wanted our discussions to be based on mutual respect.

The next day, I went into Pete's room. He was sitting down, browsing through a magazine.

"How are you doing, Pete? I asked.

"Pretty good, John. And you?"

"I am hanging in there, Pete," I said to him. "Lately, Pete, you have been coughing a lot. Don't you think it will be a good idea for you to cut down on your smoking?" I said.

"What you just said, John, is a good thing, but it is not as easy as counting one, two, three." We both laughed. "Just like you put it, for my own good, it would be reasonable to cut down on my smoking. I will try, John," he said.

"That would be a good beginning, a first step towards better health," I said.

"I would like to quit eventually, John. When you go into town, the number of places one cannot smoke is increasing. That alone says something," he added.

"That is an intelligent observation you made, Pete. It shows the health hazard posed by smoking," I said. "There is the economic side too, Pete. I don't smoke, but the residents told me the cost of a pack of cigarette is going up," I followed up.

"That is correct, John. A pack of cigarettes costs more than it used to," said Pete.

"When you kick the habit, you will be a double winner, Pete," I said to him. We both laughed.

"That is correct, John. That is very correct. I just have to find the courage. Some people call it the 'willpower' to kick the habit," said Pete.

"I wish you good luck," I said to him.

"Thank you, John."

Pete and Bud did not get along very well. The good thing was they did not share the same room. Their contact was mostly during smoke breaks in the patio at the back of the facility, in the dining room during meals, and in the dayroom, watching television. Even then, they both kept their distance from each other.

One evening, both of them were in the dayroom. A basketball game and a baseball match were on, on different channels. There were other residents in the day room. Bud and Pete were the major enthusiasts of basketball and baseball respectively. Pete changed to the baseball channel, and after about two minutes, Bud walked to the television set and changed it back to basketball. Pete would give Bud about the same amount of time and then he walked right up to the television set and switched back to baseball. It was almost a contest of will between them. Some of the other residents in the room were getting tired of it.

As if it was a burst of inspiration, Adolfo yelled, "Let's take a vote on what to watch by a show of hands. Is it going to be basketball or baseball? Those in favor of basketball, raise your hands." Seven residents raised their hands, including Bud and Adolfo. "Those in favor of baseball, raise your hands," Adolfo said. Five residents, including Pete, raised their hands.

"There you have it, Pete, the basketball fans won," said Bud. Pete was not in a conciliatory mood. He wanted a second vote. "Damn it, Pete. There was no cheating, there was nothing hidden, you were right here when the vote was taken. We live in a democracy, Pete, this is America. The majority has spoken. This is not an authoritarian society, it is not a dictatorship, this is not Russia, basketball it will be," said Bud. Bud was a voluble speaker when the occasion demanded it. The forcefulness and ardor with which he argued his case was impressive. I walked in amid his comments, and I was told what was going on. I spoke to Pete, and he calmed down. The good ending to the contest of will was that after I spoke to Pete, he did not leave the dayroom. He stayed with the rest of the residents and watched the basketball game.

*****

Although Creekside allowed sexual intercourse between consenting residents, romance between residents and staff was prohibited. It was taboo. To management, it was a no-no. There were good-looking young female residents at Creekside; there was no doubt about that. After all, Creekside was located in Santa Rosa, California. California is famous for its pretty women, amongst other things. It is the home of the stars. The girls for treatment at Creekside, though, were unavailable to employees of Creekside. As the saying goes, "you can look, but you cannot touch." As far as management was concerned, the girls for treatment at Creekside were accorded a special place; you were not to mess with them.

One Saturday morning, some minutes past nine, I was conducting rounds. I was in front of a female room. I knocked on the door, and one of the residents said, "Come in." I opened the door. There were three beds in the room. Abigail, one of the female residents in the room, was lying on her bed. The other two beds had their curtains drawn. I called out the names of the girls behind the drawn curtains, and they both answered me. I withdrew from the room with the door ajar. I took a few steps and leaned against the wall of the building directly opposite the room I just exited, cross-checking the rounds log. About three minutes later, Josh emerged from one of the drawn curtains in that same room I had walked out of, not quite four minutes. I was taken aback by the sight. I had to shake myself to be doubly sure that it was Josh coming out of the room I had just exited. He thought I had gone into another resident room to check on them. He looked at me, and I stared at him. While I was in the room conducting rounds, he was in bed with one of the female residents. The drawn curtain provided his cover. I was repulsed by what I saw. I asked myself, *what sort of a guy is he?* An imbecile, definitely an oddity. I have seen Josh go into female rooms unannounced. He did not bother to knock on the door before entering the room. When Mariam reported to me that she was stark naked when Josh walked into their room without knocking on the door, and to add insult to injury, Josh did not apologize to her, I lost all respect for the man.

Abigail, the female resident, whom I saw lying on the bed when I entered the room, came out shortly after Josh exited. I assumed that if Abigail did not see Josh entering the room, she saw him leaving. I decided to give the matter a few days. If none of the girls reported the illicit romance, I will take the case to management myself. The next day Sunday, Josh made some threatening remarks to my hearing. I ignored him. I was not one to be cowed. I was off duty on Monday, and when I came back to work on Tuesday, through the grapevine, I learned that management had been told about Josh's illicit romance last Saturday. To my surprise though, no member of management asked me any question. To be honest, I was still baffled by Josh's escapade. He thought he could get away with a quickie. Unfortunately for him, things did not work out according to his plan, if he had any. He had to pay a hefty price for his stupidity and lack of self-control. As an employee of Creekside, Josh ought to have been a custodian of good behavior and a good role model for residents. Instead, he chose to be a villain. Some of the residents at Creekside were there because they had fallen short of the norms, responsibilities, and good behavior their family members had expected of them. That Josh was foolhardy enough to engage in an illicit romance with a resident, not outside the facility, that too would have been abhorrent. But right there inside Creekside, in broad daylight, I felt, was the height of depravity and irresponsibility.

One afternoon a few weeks after this incident, at about one fifteen, rumor circulated that a staff member had turned in his resignation.

"Did you turn in your resignation, John?" Amanda asked.

"No, I did not. If I did, I would have told you," I replied.

I thought Josh may have turned in his resignation, trying to beat management before they fired him. The rumor mill was wrong. It was a firing, not a resignation that took place. A few minutes past 2:00 p.m. that same afternoon, the clinical director called a general meeting of staff. It was held in the small dining room. The clinical director was a middle-aged woman of above-average height. She was usually calm and reflective. That afternoon though, she seemed to have lost her characteristic cool. She looked visibly disturbed. General staff meetings were rare at Creekside. When it occurred, it was for specific reasons. The last general staff meeting I remembered attending was when a new health insurance policy was adopted for employees. Staff speculated as to what the meeting was about. The mood in the small dining room was charged but very quiet. It was so quiet you could hear a pin drop to the floor.

Without mincing words or beating about the bush, the clinical director went straight to the point. "Josh has been relieved of his duties. He no longer works here. I am taking no question as to why he was fired. You are not to discuss his dismissal in the presence of residents."

The meeting lasted just about fifteen minutes. To a few conscientious and objective staff, Josh's dismissal did not come as a surprise. It seemed his folly and reckless behavior finally caught up with him. Inez and Josh had been buddies. Inez was not happy Josh was fired. Later that afternoon, he walked up to me and said, "John, you are a troublemaker."

"What do you mean by that statement?" I demanded.

"Josh was fired because Ida reported she had sex with him," said Inez. "She was afraid you would report to the clinical director if she kept quiet," he added.

"Inez, do you have a conscience? Do you have principles? What Josh did was wrong, and you know it."

"Do not lecture me, John," he said.

"I am not lecturing you, Inez. I am only stating the facts you are aware of that govern this facility," I said to him.

"We will get you, John," he said.

"Do not threaten me, Inez. I do not talk much, but don't take my gentleness for weakness. I am one guy who can defend himself if I have to. If you try any shit, I will deal with you, Inez," I said to him.

As he was walking away from me, Amanda was coming out of the large dining room. She had heard my exchange with Inez.

"What is the matter, John? What did you do to Inez?" she asked.

"I did not do anything to him. I had a few words with him about Josh's termination."

"He is mad his buddy was fired," said Amanda. "They should be ashamed of themselves," she added. "Josh fooled around with female staff. He then turned around to do the same thing with female residents. He lived with Yolanda for some months, then he moved out and dumped her. He started dating Lilia. Lilia dumped him when she heard Josh was going into female residents' rooms without knocking on their doors. He got fired, he caused it himself, he got what he deserved," concluded Amanda.

Amanda was one of the objective staff members who told it like it is. She called a spade a spade.

Alcohol and drug counseling sessions were vital cores among programs offered at Creekside. Due to the prevalence of street drugs and the high rate of relapse among former residents, emphasis was placed on these programs. There was the case of Ignacio who was a model resident while at Creekside. Ignacio attended his programs religiously and stayed clean. After his discharge from Creekside, he stayed with his brother. A few months thereafter, his brother was involved in an industrial accident and was incapacitated. He could no longer care for Ignacio. Ignacio became depressed and relapsed.

During drug and alcohol sessions, residents were taught how to exercise self-discipline, staying away from people and situations that could lead them to relapse. When they were tempted, they were advised to engage in exercises that will take their mind away from the temptation, like playing lawn tennis, cycling, or running for long stretches, engaging in group activities with people who do not drink or do drugs. In sum, they were urged to engage themselves in some positive activity that would take their minds off their bitter and destructive experiences in the past.

One afternoon, after Pete came out of a session, he said to me, "John, I was touched by some of the things the counselor said during the session. He spoke a lot about the adverse and destructive effects addiction has on families. I did drugs, John.

It was out of depression caused by joblessness. I never abused my wife or kids. My in-laws might say my drug use had not come to an abusive level when my wife kicked me out. Looking back, it was a good thing she threw me out before I turned into a real drug head," he added.

"When you read the papers and listen to the news, Pete, it is scary what addiction does to families. Children are left with emotional scars that could last a lifetime. When a child cannot bond with a parent or parents because they are addicted, chances are the child might be confused about his family identity, and he or she might suffer from anxiety and emotional disorder," I said.

"I agree with you, John. I am at Creekside, trying to straighten out my life. I did not come from an alcoholic family. My parents did not smoke. They did not drink. I started drinking and smoking at age twenty-one after I left home. It was peer pressure, just to fit in," said Pete.

"This is where self-discipline comes in, Pete. This is when you have to stand your ground and maintain your individuality. In this case, it is for a good cause. It is for your own good health. If you don't like what your current friends are doing, leave them and cultivate other relationships with people whose ways of life you can cope with," I said. "This is one of the main messages the program here at Creekside tries to impart to residents."

"I know, John, you do not drink. Did you ever try it?" asked Pete.

"I tried it in college, Pete, but I couldn't handle it. Like you said earlier, it was just to fit in while hanging out with friends. A can of beer gave me headaches for hours. I decided it wasn't for me. I gave it up," I said.

"Did you ever smoke?" he asked.

"No, I never tried smoking. In the first place, I was repulsed by the smell of tobacco. Secondly, for smokers who did not practice good oral care, tobacco discolored their teeth and gave their breath a very bad odor. That too turned me off. To add to it, smoking complicates many illnesses," I said.

The following week, Adolfo and Pete, along with a handful of other residents, were in a drug rehabilitation group meeting. The meeting was always headed by a counselor. Adolfo asked for permission from the counselor to use the bathroom. He was given an ultimatum.

"I want to go to the bathroom," Adolfo said to the counselor.

"You can't leave this room at this time," said the counselor.

"My bladder is hurting me," Adolfo said.

"If you leave this meeting, you will not be allowed back in," the counselor told Adolfo.

Adolfo got up angrily and stormed out of the room. The door was locked after he left. He relieved himself in the bathroom and returned, but he was not allowed back into the meeting. He knocked on the door, but it was not opened for him.

"You son of a bitch. You want me to pee on myself? My stay here is not free. I pay money to be here," said Adolfo.

He banged on the door. He spewed more diatribe at the counselor. This went on for some minutes. The commotion was such that a doctor's visit and a staff training session were disrupted. Residents and staff rushed to the hallway to find out what the ruckus was all about.

"Calm down, Adolfo, calm down." I took him by his arm and escorted him to his room. He sat down on a chair.

"Your yelling and banging on the door will not solve your problem," I said to him.

"I asked for permission to go and use the bathroom. That son of a bitch wouldn't let me leave, so I left anyway because my bladder was hurting me," he said. "When I came back from the bathroom, he wouldn't let me in. I felt ignored. I think a dog will get a better treatment than he gave to me. It was disgusting. I am not a ten-year-old kid, John. I am a twenty-one-year-old man. He treated me like an outcast," Adolfo added.

"That regulation is tough, Adolfo. I will talk to Charge Nurse Peggy and see what she has to say," I said to him.

When the meeting was over, Pete approached me and said, "John, the rules for the meeting are very strict. Once the meeting got started, nobody is allowed to leave until it is over."

"I agree with you, Pete. I told Adolfo I will talk to Charge Nurse Peggy about it," I said.

"Hahahaha," he laughed. "That bad cop, she is part of the system. Nothing good will come out of talking to Peggy. If you had mentioned Dr. Joe, that would have sounded more reasonable," said Pete.

"Dr. Joe is on vacation. He won't be back for another two weeks," I said to Pete.

Later that day, I spoke to Charge Nurse Peggy about Adolfo and Pete's complaints.

"John, you are not new around here. You have been here for over three years. Like you know, I do not make the rules around here. I just try to enforce what the big guys in administration say," she said.

"I know Dr. Joe is on vacation. He has some pull with the big guys in administration. What about talking to him when he gets back?" I said.

"That's fine with me, John. We will talk to him when he gets back," she said.

9/11

One morning in August 2001, Amanda, looking downcast and worried, walked up to me and said, "John, I had a nightmare last night. I woke up at 3:30 a.m. in a cold sweat. I could not go back to sleep."

"Do you remember what you saw in your dream?" I asked her.

"Oh yes. Burning buildings, structures collapsing, people running helter-skelter, mass confusion. The sirens of police cars and ambulances were everywhere. It seemed the world was coming to an end," she said.

"Wow! That was quite a frightening dream. Have you had a dream in the past that became a reality?" I asked her.

"Yes. Some years ago, I dreamed my uncle was in a motor accident. I called my father on the phone and told him. It turned out my uncle was about to embark on a journey. My father asked him not to go. The two friends my uncle was to travel with proceeded with the journey. They were involved in a fatal accident. Both of them died. When my father told my uncle it was me who had warned him, my uncle sent me a thank-you card with some money."

"Oh wow! I would do the same thing. You saved his life," I said to Amanda.

Mornings at Creekside were busy. The rehabilitation department was occupied with residents, equipping them with skills that would enable them to cope with society upon their release from the facility. There were meetings between doctors, nurses, and residents. Also in the morning, some social workers met with their clients who were residents at Creekside. Creekside had only one television set. It was in the dayroom. It was usually after program hours, past noon, that a majority of the residents gathered in the dayroom to watch television.

On Tuesday, September 11, 2001, three weeks after Amanda had told me about her nightmare, a social worker handling one of our residents walked into Creekside, approached nurses' station A and said, "Have you guys heard of what is going on in New York City?"

"No, what is going on there?" asked a psychiatric technician.

"Turn on the TV. Two planes full of passengers plunged into the Twin Towers of the World Trade Center," she said.

"Whaaaat!" exclaimed the psych tech in shock. He had friends on the East Coast and had been to New York City a number of times.

"The Twin Towers of the World Trade Center are two very busy buildings weekdays," said the psychiatric technician.

We rushed to the dayroom and turned on the television. To our horror, a ghastly scene was in front of us. We were in shock.

"Is this an accident or what? Two planes crashing into two buildings within short intervals of the other?" I said.

My question was not directed to anyone in particular. It was just a reaction to a horrific scene. I left the dayroom and went in search of Amanda. I found her in a resident room, making a bed. I helped her finish making the bed, and I asked her to come with me to the dayroom. She stood in shock with her arms folded in front of the television as she watched the billowing smoke from the Twin Towers along with the chaos and confusion in the street.

"I think this is what you saw in your dream, Amanda," I said to her. "It seems you have some psychic ability, Amanda. It seems you can see into the future."

In the ensuing days, as it became clear the attackers came from Afghanistan, there was rage. Some of the high-functioning residents voiced their opinions. For the first time, Pete and Bud were in accord on the same issue.

"We are still a proud and powerful nation. Those criminals came to our country and caused such horror and destruction. If I was in my prime, I would join the army and go kick some ass in Afghanistan," said Pete in the dayroom. Everybody laughed.

"What would you do, Ramon?" asked Pete

"What those damned criminals did, like my mother used to say, is intolerable. If I was a young man, I would join the air force, fly planes to those mountains they hide in, drop some powerful bombs, and level everything. Teach them some lessons. Teach those rascals some lessons. That is what I would do," said Ramon.

"I agree with you, Ramon. We all love this country," said Pete.

"What would you do, Bud?" Pete asked.

"This is too much. There is going to be some kind of military response. Either jointly with NATO or the American government will go it alone," said Bud.

"What is NATO, Bud?" asked Adolfo.

"It is an acronym. It stands for North Atlantic Treaty Organization. It is a military alliance made up of Western countries and America."

I was impressed by Bud's response. One was reminded he was once an Ivy League student. From that day on, Adolfo nicknamed Bud "the professor."

Although it was ephemeral, politics as usual was put aside in Washington in the wake of the 9/11 attack. For the first time in a long time, the horrific events of September 11, 2001, united all Americans. Democrats, Republicans, and Independents came together as one. This show of unity was impressive. The tragedy of 9/11 brought a new spirit of togetherness to the nation. Although emotions were raw and the memory was fresh days after 9/11, that spirit of determination, pride, and defiance was evident. The American flag sold like hotcakes the week of 9/11. The nation remained undaunted, evidenced by the spike in military enlistments and people's resolve to go about their daily life and activities without fear. Lives that were lost were not forgotten. Memorial services were held in many parts of America. That spirit of unity was even extended to interfaith services in some parts of the country.

On a personal level, as the days turned into weeks, and the shock and sadness began to subside, I wondered what sort of ideology would drive someone to such dastardly acts of violence. I said to myself, *evil does exist*. Some people refuse to deal humanely with their fellow man. To such individuals, tolerance and accommodation do not exist in their vocabulary. There is that tendency to look at such individuals as evil incarnates. Human life, including their own, is worthless. They would go to any length to cause mayhem. I thought about the unspeakable atrocities that have been committed around the world. The twenty million killed in Stalin's purges and gulags, Hitler's extermination of six million Jews, the over one million lives cut short on the killing fields of Pol Pot's Cambodia, the massacres in

Rwanda, the mass killings in Srebrenica. What the perpetrators of these ugly incidents in human history had in common was hatred of their fellow man. They caused emotional trauma to their victims. They terrorized the helpless. I saw the 9/11 hijackers in the same light. They lacked empathy. With cold and cruel calculation, they carried out their wicked plot. What they did was inexcusable. History will not judge them well.

On a lighter note, the dichotomy between Charge Nurse Peggy and Pete continued unabated. According to Pete, Charge Nurse Peggy had the system behind her every move, meaning management was backing her. Pete, for his part, had his indomitable will. Pete wanted to play card with other residents. He wanted money involved. To Charge Nurse Peggy, it amounted to gambling, and she wasn't going to allow it. She told Pete cards were allowed as long as there was no money involved. There would be no gambling. Creekside was no Las Vegas, Charge Nurse Peggy maintained. Pete had other ideas. He had plans to circumvent Charge Nurse Peggy's orders. He went underground. Instead of playing cards in the day-room with residents, which was their usual rendez-vous, he resorted to playing cards in the rooms of residents who were interested in his Las Vegas-style gambling. Money exchanged hands. Nerves were frayed, and tensions mounted as some residents lost money and others were deeply indebted. This was exactly what Charge Nurse Peggy was trying to pre-vent in the first place. News reached her of what was going on, not in the dayroom but behind closed doors in residents' rooms. Charge nurse Peggy sprang into action and confronted Pete. She summoned him to her desk.

"Despite my warnings to you, Pete, that money should not be involved with card playing, you went behind my back and did it anyway," she said

"Peggy, some of the residents wanted to play cards with money involved," said Pete.

"That is not the point, Pete. The issue here is that you disregarded my advice not to get money involved with your card playing," said Charge Nurse Peggy. "I have had it with you, Pete. There will be no pass for you for the next six weeks, and if I should hear any more talk of residents losing money over cards, there will be severe consequences," she added.

"Six weeks with no pass is a very harsh punishment," Pete said to her.

"That will make you think twice before going against regulations," she countered.

Pete's Las Vegas-style gambling was outlawed. Charge Nurse Peggy asserted her authority. There was an uneasy calm between her and Pete. After three weeks of not being allowed to go on pass, Pete got edgy, irritated, and unhappy. He started to think of ways to beat Charge Nurse Peggy's ban.

"You know, Adolfo, when the mob bosses get in deep trouble, they go for plastic surgery to change their looks. How about that!" said Pete.

"You don't have the time, and you don't have the money for plastic surgery, Pete. Face reality. Let us think of something simple that would work. What about disguising as a female visitor and walk out the door just like that?" Adolfo suggested. He became an accomplice in Pete's attempt to beat Charge Nurse Peggy's refusal to issue an outing pass to Pete.

"Oh boy, that's quite an idea," said Pete.

He borrowed Dominga's oversize gown and summer hat. He donned them. He put on some makeup and topped it off with dark glasses. He asked Adolfo to go and get me. When we arrived, his door was open. He was in front of a mirror in the restroom. He turned around as we stepped in.

"What do you think, John, do I look like someone you know?" he asked.

"Where are the boobs, Pete? You like women with big boobs," said Adolfo. Pete placed his hands on his chest.

"No big deal. I will borrow Dominga's bra and fill it with a soft cloth," said Pete. I cracked up. Images of Dustin Hoffman in the movie *Tootsie* filled my mind.

"What are you trying to do, Pete?" I asked.

"I am trying to beat Peggy's ban on passes for me. I am trying to walk out the door as a female visitor," he said.

"How do you get back into the facility?" I asked.

"I will try to scale the fence. If that doesn't work, Adolfo here will let me in after midnight when all is quiet," he said.

"Why don't you save yourself some trouble and apologize to Charge Nurse Peggy. Tell her you won't do it again," I said to him.

"Do you think, John, she will accept my apology?" Pete asked.

"I think so," I said.

"I will think about it," said Pete.

The next day, Pete went to Charge Nurse Peggy and apologized.

"I want a credible witness, Pete. Go and tell John I want to see both of you," Charge Nurse Peggy said to him.

Pete came for me, and I followed him to the nurses' station.

"John, Pete came to apologize to me about card playing with money involved. I told him I want you to be my witness. Okay, Pete, offer your apology, and I will accept it," said Charge Nurse Peggy.

"I am sorry, Peggy, I will not play cards with money involved again," said Pete.

"Apology accepted. Tomorrow you will be given a pass for outing," said Charge Nurse Peggy.

When Dominga saw me later in the day, she was laughing hard. She was laughing with abandon at Pete's gimmickry.

"John, can you believe what Pete was telling me a while ago? He said that he was trying to disguise as a female visitor and sneak out but that you discouraged him from doing so. I do not think he could have pulled it off," she said.

"Anything is possible, Dominga. It is a possibility he could have pulled it off, but then he could have landed himself in big trouble," I said.

"Like how?" asked Dominga.

"For instance, during rounds, when the mental health worker conducting the rounds cannot find him. Pete's absence would lead to a thorough search of the facility, and when we cannot locate him, we will conclude that he left the building without permission. Everybody knows he cannot go on pass. That is big trouble for Pete," I said. Dominga laughed.

"What do you mean by big trouble, John?" she asked.

"In the first place, nobody knows when he left. Nobody knows where he went to. If he should get into trouble where he went to, he is on his own. In the second place, assuming he returns to Creekside safely, management will throw him out. The big guys in administration will not tolerate that kind of behavior. Thirdly, it would be very difficult for Pete to find a place to stay. Creekside will not give him a good recommendation," I said.

"I see now, John, where you are coming from when you said he will be in big trouble. I will ask Pete to thank you for discouraging him from taking the stupid action he wanted to take," said Dominga.

About a month after his apology to Charge Nurse Peggy, she told me one morning that Pete was about to be moved to a halfway house. It was a first step toward getting back into society. If it worked out for him, he could get a job someday, be self-sufficient, and get his own apartment. It was a welcome news. I was happy for Pete.

Halfway houses (homes) play a vital role in our society. The people they are trying to help get back on their feet and into society are Americans. They are sons and daughters of this great nation. They try to turn around for the better people who had been in trouble. Some of the staff at halfway houses had been in the shoes of people they are trying to help. They had suffered abuse, neglect, and deprivation themselves. They were lucky they recovered from it, straightened out their lives, and are determined to make a difference in the lives of others by helping them recover from the same wounds that they themselves had suffered from years before.

Residents at halfway houses have to abide by rules in order to stay. They need a structured environment, and halfway houses provide that structure. Some workers there have had years of counseling experience. Some even have advanced degrees in social work. Some halfway houses have consulting psychologists. There are case managers and house managers. Residents are encouraged to do their own cooking and cleaning. The housekeeping crew picks up the slack. The staff try to impart a strong instinct for survival and self-reliance to those under their care. Their success rate is far from excellent, but their effort is commendable.

Often, halfway houses encounter hostility and opposition from homeowners' associations in neighborhoods they intend to move into. The homeowners contend that their presence would constitute a blight, an eyesore so to speak, and that it would lower the value of their properties. On the other hand, it is pertinent that halfway houses are located in safe and secure neighborhoods, far removed from rough environments that would tempt residents into bad habits their counselors and managers are trying very hard to steer them away from. It makes no sense for a halfway house to be located in a neighborhood filled with drug dealers and pimps. That is not a healthy environment. Well-planned meetings between homeowners' associations and advocates of halfway houses go a long way toward resolving differences, fears, and worries. The homeowners want assurances from the halfway home advocates that there would be no trouble from the people under their care. Assurances are hard to guarantee, but halfway home staff and officials try their best to keep residents in line. Aside from observing the usual orders against alcohol, drugs, weapon possession, fighting, and the use of obscene language, residents are required to sign contracts promising to modify their behavior, abide by rules that govern the halfway house, and strive to improve themselves. Those who fall short of expectations are sent away.

The day for Pete's departure from Creekside finally arrived, it was time to leave for the halfway house. I helped him with his packing. His clothes had been laundered and tucked in his luggage the day before his departure. When the vehicle that would take him to his new abode arrived, I carried his luggage and escorted him outside to the waiting car. I placed his luggage in the boot of the car and hugged him.

"Take good care of yourself," I said to him.

"Thanks, John, for all your help," he said.

You are welcome, Pete," I said.

He got into the car, and the driver took off. As the vehicle was leaving Creekside, I was saying to myself, *I hope Pete will make it. I hope he will be one of Creekside's success stories.*

FREEDOM

Freedom, my ability to choose.
Freedom, my ability to speak my
mind, without fear of reprisal.
Freedom, my ability to make my
own decisions. I may not be right
all the time, the decisions are mine.
Freedom, my ability to act within the
confines of the law.
Freedom, my unfettered access
to whatever destination I may choose.
If I had the wings of an eagle, I would
fly over the mountain.

I reflected on the issues raised by Anna and Adolfo. I thought about freedom, respect, and human dignity. Anna had spoken about freedom, her desire to do her own thing without officialdom. Adolfo had raised the issues of respect and human dignity when he challenged Creekside's unwritten but implied policy of not letting out residents once counseling sessions were underway, until the end of deliberations.

Freedom

Freedom encompasses and recognizes the rights of the majority and the minority in society. Freedom is laden with choices every individual must make for himself or herself. Freedom builds an enlightened society. You are not led by the nose; you are able to think for yourself. One of the ideals inherent in a free society is that you not only learn from your own mistakes but you learn from the mistakes of other people. In a free society, each individual might decide on his or her own boundary, the point beyond which they earnestly believe that institutional or societal values are at variance with their own core beliefs.

For example, safety and orderliness should not be purchased at the price of losing one's privacy, dignity, freedom of speech, and freedom of choice. When we surrender our freedom of speech and freedom of choice, there is that tendency to look at people around us with paranoid distrust. It is true that regulation is necessary for the smooth functioning of a large society. It should, however, not come at the expense and inconvenience of individuals in the society by way of oppressive and draconian rules and regulations.

During wartime, however, things are different. Freedom could be restricted for the good of society and country. War could mean more freedom for some and less freedom for others. During the Second

World War, American women played a vital role in society. They took on jobs performed by men since lots of them had gone off to war. These women were working in the fields of manufacturing and shipbuilding. Since they were performing manly jobs, it was natural that they demanded the same pay given to men. It was an expansion of their freedom, and the women loved it. On the other hand, for Japanese living in America, the war meant less freedom. Since it was the Japanese government that bombed Pearl Harbor in December 1941, an obvious act of aggression, the American government, with good reason, did not look with favor on the Japanese population in America. There was good reason for distrust, sabotage being one of them. They could turn into saboteurs who could undermine the American government with insidious activities. A vast number of them living in the country were rounded up and put in detention camps. Communists and communist sympathizers had the harshest treatment. They were hauled off to jail and put on trial. They were looked upon as despicable individuals not worthy of an ounce of sympathy. They were the very antithesis of what the American government stood for and believed in. They were considered a threat to the social order in America.

Respect

Society functions better when respect is equally bestowed on everybody regardless of color, gender, or race. People's perspective on respect might differ, but put in a simple way, respect can be defined as a regard for the feelings, wishes, and rights of other people. It can also mean an appreciation of the value of something tangible. Respect is a virtue cherished universally. Each of us desires not only to embody respect but also to receive it. Respect encompasses what we say and the way we act. Showing others that you take their feelings and thoughts into consideration is the way to earn their respect. When you show respect to others through appropriate words and actions, they in turn will respond positively and listen to your opinions and views. One of the key ingredients in building self-esteem is respect. Respect plays a role in our daily lives. In the offices, restaurants, and stores we frequent daily, the orderliness and smooth transactions displayed in those places are reflections of respect. At the post office, you wait for your turn to be served. At the doctor's office, you wait to be called. At the bill-paying office, you do the same thing.

In schools, it is paramount that mutual respect is demonstrated between students and teachers. Students ought to listen to their teachers and do their best in class. Teachers, for their part, will earn the respect and accolades of their students when they provide quality education and respect their students as individuals. Creativity in presenting their academic work to their students will enhance the teacher's standing.

Respect is priceless. Respect and honor are synonymous. In some societies, a man's respect or honor cannot be bought or traded. You have to earn it. In such places, your conduct and speech play a role in the amount of respect you garner in the community.

Kids, at an early age, are taught respect. Respect for their parents and family members, respect for the people they deal with outside the family. They are taught to say "thank you" for gifts and courtesies extended to them. Classmates at school, friends on the playing field—respect is accorded to them by the harmonious interactions between them.

Respect begets further respect. For other people to respect you, you have to respect them as well. Just like charity begins at home, respect begins with self-respect. It then extends to the respect of other people.

Human dignity

Human nature plays a role in human dignity. Human dignity may be defined as the state of being worthy of honor or respect. Human nature could be something we were born with, something innate, something present on the day of our birth. The environment we were brought up in and the inter-actions we had while growing up form part of who we become. Right-thinking people everywhere want to live a dignified life. They want to be seen in the eyes of their fellow man as worthy of respect and honor. They make a conscious decision to uphold themselves with dignity by way of exemplary con-duct and are appalled when they meet with churlish treatment.

Maltreatment and debasement give rise to timid-ity, insecurity, and hostility. Disquietude and rest-lessness become constant companions of the vic-tim of such a callous treatment. Such a fellow sees himself or herself as the victim of his or her fellow man's inhumanity. The revolts that erupt occasion-ally in some parts of the world, especially in dicta-torial societies, are attempts to restore some mea-sure of human respect and human dignity. It is not easy to recover from the scars inflicted by such ill treatment. Somebody strong might recuperate and function in a healthy manner in society. The feeble and weak-minded could succumb and degenerate into melancholy. Such a person might suffer from mental torment. It would be reasonable to say that such a fellow would become spiteful and malignant, swollen with venom, and filled with hatred for his or her abuser.

Imagine being dismissed by your fellow man as a pariah and an outcast, an object of loathing and ridicule. One is ignored, spurned, and reviled, bespattered with the mud of disdain. You are found ignoble and repulsive without an explainable course. This is a passage through fire, so to speak. This can be considered a brutish treatment of a sensitive human being. Adolfo found himself in such a position.

We, as human beings, react differently to situations. Some people are endowed with the strength and fortitude to ride out callous and dehumanizing circumstances. Late President Nelson Mandela of South Africa definitely belonged in this category. For years, he withstood the beastly and very debasing treatment meted out to him by the then-apartheid regime of South Africa. For twenty-seven years, Nelson Mandela was incarcerated. He was denied his freedom. When he came out of prison after twenty-seven years of abuse and maltreatment, he chose peace and reconciliation with his jailers. A lesser man would have wanted to settle scores with his enemies. That is the measure of who Nelson Mandela was. Not everybody has the courage and forgiving spirit of Nelson Mandela.

There is that plausible argument that human nature cannot be legislated. We all have the need for the restroom occasionally. Adolfo needed to go to the restroom, he asked in good faith and manner for permission to go and use the restroom, he was confronted with a look of disgust by the counselor in charge of the meeting. Adolfo saw himself as an object of loathing. When he insisted on going to use the restroom, he was given an ultimatum. Adolfo felt disrespected and the counselor's conduct undignified. Although he felt shunned and that whispers of aversion from the counselor would follow him, Adolfo summoned up the courage to do what he felt was right for him at that particular time. He wasn't going to pee on himself, Adolfo maintained. Out of frustration and pressure from the urgent need to urinate, he stormed out of the meeting.

Intolerance does rear its ugly head individually and institutionally. On the other hand, the benefit of being sensitive to tolerance is the ability to put ourselves in the shoes of the other guy. When a conscious effort is made to understand the other person's feelings and needs, there is that likelihood we will understand ourselves better and function well in society. Right-thinking people everywhere believe that respect for the dignity and well-being of each member of society, whether within or outside an institution, is the logical foundation for freedom, justice, and peace. In situations like Creekside, I strongly hold the opinion that serious efforts should be made to accommodate and protect people who are psychologically or mentally impaired or challenged. Humane considerations in dealing with the mentally impaired or challenged do a lot of good toward their healing. My four-year stay at Creekside taught me that lesson. The influence of a good person lives on in the kindness he or she shows to others, especially the powerless in society. You can turn around somebody's life for the better by being gentle and kind in the way you deal with them.

After Pete's departure for the halfway house, there was a lull at Creekside among the residents. Adolfo and Dominga were closest to him. They missed him more than any other resident. For Charge Nurse Peggy, it was a breath of fresh air and a sigh of relief. It seemed as if a heavy burden had been lifted off her shoulders. That feeling of relief did not last long though. About a month after Pete left for the halfway house, a new resident named Lucas was admitted to Creekside. Lucas and Pete were direct opposites.

While Pete was direct and sometimes confrontational, Lucas was sneaky, and some of his actions he saw as pranks were annoying. Lucas was a petite man with red hair, a mischievous smile, and deceiving looks. Behind his calm appearance lurked a miscreant who could unleash a startling punch or an unnerving pinch to an unsuspecting staff member or resident.

Lucas was born premature. He was adversely affected by the birth and the oxygen given to him after birth. His mother was said to have been stressed, exhausted, and sick all through Lucas's period of gestation. The doctors and nurses thought Lucas would not make it. He was in an incubator for several weeks. He had severe limitations. His speech was muddled, his articulation was very slow. As the years passed and Lucas's mental and physical incapacities became apparent, his parents abandoned him. Lucas was taken to a foster home.

Lucas's pranks were sometimes amusing, at other times, off-the-wall. On a routine rounds check, a mental health worker searched for Lucas and could not find him. To add to the mental health worker's confusion, he looked at the outing log, and Lucas was not signed out. Charge Nurse Peggy was told about Lucas's missing status. She summoned his roommate and inquired if he had seen him.

"That guy is weird. Check underneath his bed. He may be lying underneath his bed," declared the roommate.

The mental health worker went back to their room, bent down under Lucas's bed, and to his surprise and wonder, Lucas was lying underneath his bed.

"What are you doing underneath your bed?" asked the mental health worker.

"I am playing hide-and-seek," he said.

He wiggled out like a snake and was grinning like a witless fellow.

Out of confusion or sheer prank, Lucas walked into a female resident's room and lay on her bed. He was in the wrong room and in the wrong bed. The door to the room was wide open. Lucas always left his door open. The female resident walked into her room and was surprised to find Lucas on her bed.

"You are in the wrong room and in the wrong bed," declared the female resident.

"This is my room and my bed," Lucas said.

"Is this your picture? Are these your gowns?" the female resident asked. "You are one scatterbrain," she added.

Convinced that the room was not his, Lucas stood up and was taken to his room.

Early one morning, Lucas was found showering in the female shower room. He was redirected by a bemused housekeeper who was flabbergasted and could not contain her laughter. For me, it was hard to determine whether it was a case of severe mental retardation or confusion brought on by the medications he was plied with daily. Lucas sometimes wore his clothes inside out. "Lucas, you are wearing the wrong side of your shirt," a resident would correct him.

"No, it is the vogue. Have you heard Madonna's song "Vogue"? That is what it is. It is the vogue," he maintained.

Sometimes, Lucas would walk up to a resident and say to him, "Do you want to see my bad boy posture?" He would contort his face, clasp his hands, and get into a boxing posture. "When you see me in this mood, I am mad, don't mess with me. I am ready to do damage to my opponent," he would say. Lucas's pranks and antics were tolerated for some time. It was when he started spanking the female residents on their butt it was decided it was time to take him elsewhere. Lucas's departure was speedily arranged after he sneaked up on a female resident and grabbed her ass as she was about to enter the small dining room. The female resident reported her displeasure and embarrassment to a staff who then took the matter to Charge Nurse Peggy. Lucas's behavior had become intolerable. He had to be taken to another facility. A few days after he harassed the female resident, Lucas was taken to a different place.

*****

Pete seemed to have turned into a party animal after his release from Creekside. This was his way of letting out his frustrations for not being able to see his children. A staff at the halfway house where Pete was staying saw him partying with teenagers old enough to be his kids. Pete was seen outside a pub with boys in baggy pants, T-shirts, white canvas shoes, and many cans of beer. This was not the type of crowd befitting a man who wanted to stay sober. Some of the boys were making noise for the wrong reasons. They were obviously drunk. They were yelling and whistling wildly to a group of girls nearby.

One of the boys was celebrating his birthday. He seemed too drunk to keep a proper hold on himself and enjoy the company of his friends. Two of his friends succeeded in talking him into getting into a car and having some rest.

It turned out Pete and some of the youths he was partying with had something in common. Some of the boys were unemployed. Just like Pete was trying to hide his frustrations with booze, the unemployed youths were trying to mask their unhappiness for not having a job with wild parties and drunkenness. If only temporarily, their feelings of dejection were soothed. Pete and the unemployed youths found temporary relief from booze. A teetotaler who was unemployed might wonder how downing large quantities of beer would help one's cause, would help toward one's goal which was finding a job. Excessive drinking and wild partying, a teetotaler would contend, would not help the goal of finding gainful employment. On the other hand, people differ in their personalities. People seek various ways and means of solving their problems.

Pete was keeping late nights and running afoul of rules and regulations in his place of abode. Curfew at the halfway house started at 9:00 p.m., but Pete sometimes got back after 10:00 p.m. There was no cogent and plausible reason for his keeping late nights. If Pete had a job that kept him late outside, that would have been excusable. Pete had no job, no valid reason for keeping late nights, and his problem was compounded by the lame arguments he had with the staff at the halfway house. Pete could not see his kids, and he had no job. That was cause for unhappiness, but he did not help himself by going overboard and behaving recklessly. A more mature approach would have helped his cause.

Pete would have sought help with regard to seeing his kids. He loved his kids, and he missed them—there was no doubt about that. He would have spoken to officials at the halfway house who would then make arrangements to talk to his wife about visitation rights with his kids. Pete's wife had strong family support, and they might insist on some conditions. They might stipulate that he gets a job first before he could see his kids. That would be a good sign to them that Pete was on a serious path to recovery. It was a possibility too that his wife's family members might not want the kids alone with their father. They might insist on a third party during their visitation. Pete's downward spiral into drunkenness and drugs left the family with a bitter experience, and his wife was determined to shield the kids from it. For the good and welfare of the kids, some conditions might be put forward by his wife's family before Pete could visit with his kids.

Looking at the situation from a positive standpoint, such a condition might be a stimulus for Pete to sit up, discipline himself, and do the right thing. Unfortunately for Pete, he did not take that route. He never took any initiative that would start a dialogue with his wife about the possibility of visitation with his kids. He hurt himself further with his intransigence and wayward behavior toward officials at the halfway house. The staff had no choice but to turn him loose. Pete was at the halfway house for six months. His six months absence from Creekside seemed like an eternity. Charge Nurse Peggy was told Pete was coming back to Creekside, but she was not updated on Pete's physical condition. She told us Pete was coming back, and we knew that was not good news.

When Pete arrived at Creekside, we were surprised by his physical appearance. He was not looking good. It was not the man who had left us six months earlier that we got back. Pete came back frail. He had lost a lot of weight. His hair was bushy. So was his beard. He was unkempt, his gait was slow. He could still crack jokes though, which was comforting. Dominga and Adolfo were shocked by the sudden change in Pete's physical appearance. So were Charge Nurse Peggy and myself. We wondered what the problem was. Pete seemed to have aged ten years in the past six months. Although Charge Nurse Peggy was not thrilled by the hard times Pete gave to her, his sudden change and the deterioration in his health were a source of concern to her.

Even residents who were not close to him and were not enamored of him noticed the changes in him. Before he left, Pete used to spend long hours in the dayroom playing cards and socializing with residents. He now spent lots of time in his room by himself, most of the time sleeping. When he woke up, he complained of pains. I sometimes reminded him of his meal, which was a rarity. Pete's appetite was good before he left. Now he picked at his meal and barely ate a fraction of the food on his plate. He would eat a tiny fraction of his meal and say he could eat no more, he was full. Sometimes he said he was constipated, and there was no improvement in his weight. Pete complained of fatigue and pain and sometimes could not keep food down in his stomach. At such times, he would use the restroom a few minutes after eating.

Pete was getting weaker. He could no longer perform his activities of daily living. I helped him with his shaving and shower, and I did his laundry for him. Pete's deterioration was a real source of worry. Most of the doctors who visited Creekside were psychiatrists, not medical doctors. After some lengthy conversation between the clinical director and Charge Nurse Peggy, it was decided that Pete should be taken to the hospital to see a medical doctor. He was told of the decision, and it was okay with Pete. Arrangements were made, and Pete was taken to the hospital to see the doctor. He was there for some days. Examinations and tests were performed on him. When the results of those tests came out, it was heartbreaking. The news was devastating. The doctors concluded Pete had cancer. It was not caught on time, and he had a few months to live. It was as if harrowing news had been delivered to a family member. A feeling of dismay and anguish hung in the air at Creekside as the news broke. Man is mortal. Even the bravest among us, when we remember that we will one day die, are humbled.

The doctors were told about Pete's status as regards his wife. They were told Pete was in contact with his wife but that they were not enamored of each other. The question then arose how best to communicate Pete's condition to his family, especially the kids. The doctors wanted to know if the couple were divorced.

"No" came the answer from Charge Nurse Peggy. "They were separated," she added.

"It is still a nuclear family then. They are still regarded as a social unit," said the doctor on the phone. "Pete said you have his family's phone number, is that correct?" asked the doctor.

"That is correct," said Charge Nurse Peggy.

"Let me have the number, and I will tell his wife about her husband's condition. I will tell her to be careful and to have some support around her when she breaks the news to the kids and the rest of the family," said the doctor.

When the news of Pete's terminal cancer was conveyed to his wife, she broke down and sobbed. It was a shocker. Nobody saw it coming. Her kids were not home when she got the bad news. They were visiting friends. Later that night, she decided she had to let the kids and the rest of the family know about what had befallen them, about Pete's condition, the next day. When Charge Nurse Peggy called and asked her why she would not let Pete see the kids, she said, "I wanted him to get a job and keep it, show signs he was ready to be a good family man, able to provide for his kids. I never knew it would come to this."

I asked myself what would be the definition of a good family man. One who is a good example for his kids, be there for them in times of good and bad. A man who would be able to comfort his kids and stand up for them, provide basic necessities for them. To Pete's wife, he was never there for the kids. He did not step up when they needed him, and the pain the kids suffered as a result tore at her heart. From her perspective, Pete failed the kids. There was no other way of putting it.

Nora and Pete met at a friend's house in Oakland. She had just moved from the South. Her folks thought she was crazy coming out to California. She loved it though when she got to the West Coast. She was introduced to Pete by her friend. With Pete being the voluble type, they got engrossed in conversation. Nora quickly found out that her mother and Pete had something in common. They both could entertain people with animated conversations. She developed a fondness for Pete, and they started dating. Pete took Nora to the beach, and she found the Pacific Ocean beautiful and peaceful. Nora developed an affection for the ocean, and they made several trips to the beach after their first visit.

Pete had a good sense of humor. He made Nora laugh, and she liked that. She had never met a well-intentioned boyfriend before Pete came her way. Guys she had dated before Pete were all about sex. They wanted to get laid. Nora wanted a relationship, and Pete was willing to offer her that. She liked what she saw in Pete, the tone of his voice, the tender smile on his face during their conversations, the feel of his hands when he touched her.

Pete had a close friend who owned a successful tree service and landscaping business in Oakland. Nobody Pete knew threw a party quite like his friend. Pete's friend was a party animal. Pete and Nora were invited to his friend's Fourth of July cookout party. They had been dating for eight months by then. There were lots of people at the party held at Pete's friend big house with a spread-out backyard. The guests were of all ages, ranging from youngsters who played with each other to adults who gathered in small groups, holding conversations and sipping wine. Pete and his friend manned the barbecue. There was plenty to eat and drink. Guests had a good time. They were pleased and happy. When the party was over, Nora was happy with what she saw and experienced; she was impressed. On their way home, Pete asked Nora what she wanted in life. After some minutes of silence, she said she wanted a happy family of her own like the one she came from, a husband and kids. Pete told her that her response was reasonable, adding that most people wanted happiness in their lives.

After eighteen months of dating, Pete proposed to Nora, and she accepted. Nora had a couple of girl-friends. Some were happy for her. One of her friends was skeptical. The skeptical friend told Nora that she had the instinctive feeling Pete was not the right guy for her. Something about Pete did not quite add up, she warned. Nora had fallen head over heels for Pete, so she turned a deaf ear to her friend's warning. She was charmed by Pete's sense of humor and easy-going ways. Nora felt that Pete was a solid and reliable guy who would take good care of her and treat her well. The eighteen months Pete had dated her had not produced any surprises. Pete had a full-time job, he took her out, and he brought her gifts. Pete wasn't cheating on her. She liked that. Pete's friends and acquaintances did not have anything ugly to say about him. Nora's parents were faithful to each other and had been married for over twenty-three years. She hoped she would have the same good luck as her mother with a long and successful marriage.

Their wedding was simple and was held at a local church. The couple was dressed modestly. Nora wore a simple lace dress and carried a bouquet of red roses. Pete wore a black suit. Nora's father gave her away. A reception for invited friends was held at the spacious home of Pete's friend. Their wedding was a first step toward establishing a family.

Family, to billions of people around the world, implies a place you can call a home. A place you can return to after travel, a place you can go away from at your own choosing and come back to when you so desire. Family, to most people, implies a comfort zone, a place of beginning and probably where one ends his or her life's journey.

Nora was some weeks pregnant when she and Pete were joined in matrimony. They moved in together in an apartment the night of their wedding. She told Pete she had missed her period and that she suspected she was pregnant. Morning sickness followed shortly after their wedding. She had flu-like symptoms in the morning. Pete had mixed emotions. He was excited and nervous at the same time, which is typical of most first-time fathers. After nine months of gestation, Nora went into labor. It was her first pregnancy. It wasn't easy. She was in a great deal of pain. She screamed a lot in the delivery room, and with the worried look on Pete's face, the doctors and nurses decided to send him out of the delivery room.

Pete paced the hospital corridor nervously, wearing pajamas and a gown, with a shower cap on his head. After about six hours of labor, Nora delivered their first child. It was a healthy baby boy who weighed almost nine pounds. It was a big relief when a nurse came out of the delivery room and announced to Pete that he was the father of a healthy baby boy. Pete was handed his son a few minutes after the announcement, the lad was wrapped in a tiny bundle, and Pete was quick to note that the boy looked like him. He pulled his son to his chest and gave thanks silently in his mind. Pete knew he had responsibilities to his wife and son. The first hurdle had been cleared though. Mother and child were okay.

Nora's parents were high school sweethearts whose love for each other blossomed into marriage. Her father was a cool-headed and warmhearted man who did not talk much, a man who never said a word he did not mean and never promised anything he could not deliver. While growing up, Nora never heard any threats, verbal or physical abuse from her father. He was the type of man who sat people down when he had differences with them, including members of his own family, talked to them, and sorted out differences amicably.

As opposed to her father, who was taciturn, Nora's mother was a good conversationalist, who kept discussions running in smooth and well-worn channels. She got along with ease with most people, including her in-laws. While they were growing up, their mother stayed at home and kept a tight rein on her kids. Their mother went to work after the baby in the family had started schooling. Those years of caring, devotion, and paying attention to her kids yielded good dividends. Mom and dad were not alienated. It was a close-knit family.

Although Nora's father was cool and gentle, he was firm when it came to disciplining his kids. Nora and her two brothers and sister got along fairly well, but when differences cropped up, it was skillfully handled by her parents. Once in a while, when disputes got heated among the siblings, her father's demeanor and instructions left no room for ambiguity; the kids had to fall in line. If the kids had objections to what they were asked to do, complaints had to be lodged after the completion of the task assigned to them. This was the kind of family Nora grew up in, a home where, at an early age, discipline and responsibility were implanted in the kids. Mom and dad had a relationship based on mutual respect which extended to the kids. On weekdays, the family kitchen was the rendezvous for her mother, her two brothers, her sister, and herself. After their evening meal and the completion of their homework, their mother told them tales about her folks, after which she asked each of them how their day had gone. The kids were usually in bed when their father got home from work.

Weekends, after the kids had taken care of their chores, her father sat down with their mother and the kids, talking about what they had done all week. It was the weekends Nora's father played catch-up with his kids since he came home late weekdays.

If there was something important for him to know about the kids during the week, his wife filled him in. One family member's problem was the whole family's problem. They took the attitude that a problem halved was a problem on its way to a resolution. By opening up and sharing each other's concerns, potential problems that would have had disastrous consequences if they had been hidden were nipped in the bud.

The family resided in a town where Christmas tree lighting ceremony was a tradition. Each December, various families decorated the trees lining some of the local commercial houses downtown. Each family decorated with their favorite colors. The tree-lighting ceremony was presided over by the mayor. A local church provided the choir that supplied the Christmas carols. On the set date, at approximately 8:00 p.m., families gathered downtown. Sometimes the crowd was so large that some families stood on sidewalks. With a signal from the mayor by raising his right hand, the Christmas trees came alive in twinkling colored lights with sparks leaping amid their branches. Applause from the gathered crowd filled the night air, and the choir began singing Christmas carols. Families exchanged greetings for a merry Christmas and a happy new year. There were hugs, handshakes, and kind regards for a healthy, happy, and prosperous new year.

Early Christmas morning, amid Christmas carols supplied by the family's entertainment center and good cheer, Nora's family spent some time opening their presents and expressing gratitude for what they received. Gift exchanges were followed by Christmas breakfast, usually biscuits, sausages, and bacon, the family favorite. Christmas dinner was always a hearty meal. Nora's father made the stuffing, her mother cooked the turkey, Nora took care of the vegetables. Her brothers made the potatoes and the whipped cream. The whipped cream was for the dessert, usually apple and pumpkin pies at the end of the Christmas dinner. The family was always regaled with good food, which they were thankful for. At the end of the meal, everyone was stuffed up and reluctant to move. They would start teasing each other about who could shed the added pounds faster after the holidays. Such was the type of home Nora came from, a close-knit and happy family. Unfortunately for her, she had to find out individual stars are aligned differently. Her fate was different from that of her mother. What was true for one person was not always the case for another person. Each individual had their own separate journey to make. Nora was not as successful as her mother when it came to marriage.

There was some soul-searching when Pete's illness came to light. Where did the ball drop? Why wasn't his cancer caught on time? There was no sign of illness when he left Creekside six months ago. When the inevitable was accepted, all efforts were concentrated on keeping Pete comfortable. I helped him with his shower every other day, I fed him when he was too weak to feed himself, and I laundered his clothes for him when they were dirty. Some days he was strong enough to help himself. At other times, he was so weak he could hardly do anything for himself. Pete was thirsty one night. As he was trying to get out of bed to get some water, somehow he lost his balance and fell down. He was so weak he could not stand up on his own. Nobody knew how long he layed on the floor. It was when his roommate wanted to use the restroom that he saw Pete on the floor and helped him up. The roommate then told the night-shift workers. Fortunately, Pete did not break any bones. He had a minor laceration on his face.

At the urging of Charge Nurse Peggy, Pete's wife agreed that his kids would come and visit with him. They had to come and say their final goodbye. The kids came to see Pete a few days after Charge Nurse Peggy had spoken to their mother. There were two boys. They looked like their father. A superficial observer would confuse them for twins. They had been told of their father's illness and that he was not going to recover. At fourteen and sixteen years old, it was daunting news they had to struggle with.

What was remarkable about Pete was that he was not afraid of death. There was no anxiety, no emotional outburst. He had accepted his fate, his own finality, calmly. His only regret was not being able to see his boys grow up.

It was an emotional visit, but Pete was determined there would be no tears shed in the presence of his boys. He had to be strong for his kids. His attitude was there was nothing he could do about his illness now. He had accepted his fate and was at peace with himself. His kids' red and watery eyes conveyed the unspoken words and emotions held in check. They knew this was the last time they would see their father alive. I met with Pete's boys briefly, but from all Pete had told me about them when the going was good, it seemed as if I had known them for a long time. I was touched by their pain. I felt for them. They were devastated. The agony on their faces told the whole story; it was palpable. The loss they knew was coming was immeasurable. There was an eerie silence in the room for a few minutes, as if each person was trying to absorb the impact of what was about to happen.

I was wondering how they were going to handle the cruel blow life was about to hand out to them. Lately, Pete had not been around and had not been of help to them. At least they knew they had a father who was alive, and they remembered the good times they had with him when all was well. There was that possibility that while Pete was alive and healthy, things could turn around for the better. Unfortunately, that was not the case. They were going to be fatherless soon. Death was lurking in the corner and about to snatch their father away from them. If Pete did not have the bad luck of working for a company that closed its plants and moved production overseas, maybe he would have been healthy and around to care for his family. If he had worked for a good establishment with decent health insurance, maybe his cancer would have been detected on time and nipped in the bud. These were some of the thoughts that ran through my mind.

After two hours of visitation, Pete's kids hugged him and left. Pete started sobbing after their departure. I went in and stayed with him for half an hour. I held his hands and comforted him. I handed him tissues from his bedside table. "I would have loved to see my boys turn into adults. I am not that lucky," he said. Tears started rolling down from his eyes, and I had tears in my eyes too. It was a sad comment but a true and a very painful moment for both of us. There was nothing both of us could do or anybody could do to arrest the ugly situation Pete was faced with. Death was knocking on the door, so to speak. On the other hand, I said to myself, *Pete's passing on, his absence from the scene, might have a positive impact on his kids.* I envisioned his boys growing up fast, taking responsibility for themselves and their actions. I envisioned their mother impressing upon them that the world is a village, that failure is an orphan and has no friend, but success has a family and many friends. I envisioned Nora urging her boys to make the most of a bad situation and make a success of themselves.

A mean-minded person would think that Charge Nurse Peggy would be gleeful about Pete's bad prognosis, given the very contentious relationship they had for almost a year. That was not the case. On the contrary, Pete's terminal illness brought Charge Nurse Peggy close to him. It mellowed her. She was instrumental in arranging the visitation between Pete and his kids. When on duty, she was always checking on him to see how he was doing. She asked me to do whatever was needed to keep him comfortable. In a strange but interesting way, impending death had brought two former antagonists together. The differences between them were bridged, the alienation of previous months was forgotten, a silent accord was reached. Pete's terminal illness brought closure to disputes and forged an understanding between Charge Nurse Peggy and himself.

It is gratifying to note how unforeseen and unfortunate events bring out compassion in humans. When it was decided Pete had to be moved to a hospice, he gave his personal belongings to Charge Nurse Peggy for safekeeping until his wife came for them. This would have been unthinkable a few months ago. This was the same woman Pete had once dubbed "a bad cop."

Pete was moved to a hospice a few days after his kids had visited him. At hospices, there is a shared sense of empathy. Hospices are better equipped to handle the terminally ill in a more dignified way that diminishes suffering until they pass on. From what the doctors said, we knew Pete did not have much time left. News reached us that Pete had died four weeks after he was transferred to the hospice. The information had been given to his wife. There was a subdued atmosphere at Creekside when we got the news. It seemed as if a family member had died. Pete was a resident at Creekside. The sorrow and feelings of anguish were genuine. On the other hand, I thought of when Pete woke up from sleep and was in a great deal of pain. There was no more pain for Pete. He was at peace at last. The trials and tribulations he had gone through were a thing of the past.

Pete's wife and family members had to make funeral arrangements. A casket had to be chosen. A service and minister to preside over it had to be arranged for. On the day of the funeral, Adolfo, Dominga, Anna, and two other residents attended. The presiding minister made a short statement and read from the Bible. Pete's body was cremated, and his ashes were spread over the Pacific Ocean.

"Our spokesman is gone. Somebody has to step up to the plate," declared Anna.

She was correct. Pete did speak out on some of the issues that affected the residents.

"We will remember him for his sense of humor," said Dominga.

Even in his waning health, Pete did keep his sense of humor. One day I asked him what I could do for him.

"Let's have a wild party with some dancing girls in bikinis!" he said.

Pete said "good morning" to Dr. Joe one afternoon at about 2:30 p.m.

"It is almost three in the afternoon, Pete," said Dr. Joe.

"It is morning in some part of the world, Doc," said Pete.

They both started laughing. Such was his sense of humor. It was contagious.

All of mankind believe life will come to an end someday. Nothing is forever, including human life. This is a universal belief. There is no argument about death. It could be at a young age, it could come at old age, but one thing is certain—death will surely come someday. It is one trait all of mankind have in common. Death does not respect anybody. It does not matter what your station in life is, how high or low your standing in society is. It does not matter whether you are rich or poor, strong or weak. The strange part is nobody knows when that time will come.

We have heard stories about people who went out for a ten-minute errand and never made it back home alive. We have heard stories about people who complained of a mere headache the previous night and were found dead on their bed the next morning. Life is short and full of uncertainties.

Life is a journey, it has been said. A journey no one knows exactly when or how it is going to end. All one can hope for is how to make the uttermost use of one's time during that journey. Death is inevitable. It is a debt we all owe. During funerals and trips to cemeteries, we reflect on the life of the deceased with the full knowledge that one day, it will be our corpse pallbearers would be carrying on that same road we once trod. After some pensive moments pondering Pete's death, I consoled myself with these words from Julius Caesar:

> Cowards die many times before their
> deaths. The valiant never taste of
> death but once. Of all the wonders
> that I yet have heard, it seems most
> strange to me that men should fear,
> seeing that death, a necessary end,
> will come when it will come.

Charge Nurse Peggy seemed to have struck a peaceful and harmonious note with Pete's wife during their conversations. A rapport developed between the two women. There were several substantive discussions between Charge Nurse Peggy and Nora after Pete's death. Pete's wife worried about her kids. For all practical purpose, she was now a single parent. She was now the mother and "father" of her two boys. Despite the outward loathing of Pete by his wife, understandably due to his bad behavior, deep down in her heart, she was hoping Pete would turn a new leaf. She was hoping Pete would come back to his old self, come back to the man he used to be and once again be the head of the family. Pete's sudden illness and death was a real shocker. It was a hard blow to his wife, and she was knocked down by the tragedy. After the funeral, Pete's wife came for his belongings. It was heartwarming to see the face behind the soft voice we heard over the phone. She was calm. She bore her sorrow with dignity.

For some time, Pete's wife, with help from her family, had been coping with the responsibilities for the kids, making up for their father's absence, and it seemed she was doing a good job. In the back of her mind though, she was hoping Pete would come back and help her. His death was a monumental setback for his wife.

"With your husband's death, there will be some down days. There will be some difficult times, but life has to go on," Charge Nurse Peggy told her. "Pete's death might have a positive outcome. His kids might grow up fast, be independent and self-reliant. It seemed there was no other choice. They had to do it for their own good," Charge Nurse Peggy said to Nora.

Charge Nurse Peggy urged her not to dwell on her sorrow but to go out and do something with the kids. "Go to the movies, go bowling, go for long walks on the beach, and talk about things that interest the kids and you. Do things with the kids that would cheer them up and put them in a bright and happy mood. Despite the unforeseen tragedy that has befallen the family, life has to go on," Charge Nurse Peggy advised Nora.

Pete had told us that his wife was a hard worker. She sometimes worked two jobs. "Go on with your work, but take care of the kids, keep them active, and happy. You have to be strong for your kids," Charge Nurse Peggy counseled Nora. "It will be a while before you get over what has happened, but you will get over it. You were married to Pete for seventeen years. That is not something you are going to get over in a few weeks," Charge Nurse Peggy told Nora. "Invest your time and energy in your kids. You will be happy for it," Charge Nurse Peggy urged her.

"After your period of mourning, at a point, you are convenient and confident in yourself, you might start thinking of beginning a new life. Start dating, and possibly find a new mate," she told Nora. "Your kids are fourteen and sixteen years old. Before you know it, they will be grown and be out of the house. Don't be alone. Don't be by yourself when they are gone," she counseled Nora. "Find someone who likes kids and can get along with them. When the kids are grown and out of the house, you have someone you love you can share your life with. With time, things will get better. Time has a way of healing wounds and soothing pains," Charge Nurse Peggy counseled Nora. Pete's wife thanked her and told her she would keep in touch.

Peggy was genuinely concerned about Pete's wife and the kids. She extended a hand of friendship to the family. Her advice and suggestions were given in good faith, and she asked Pete's wife to call her anytime she wanted to talk. If there was anything she could do for the family to lessen their burden, she was willing to help.

Santa Rosa is approximately fifty miles north of San Francisco, in Sonoma County. It is located in the Sonoma wine country. Visitors to San Francisco often include Santa Rosa in their itinerary. The city is in a unique location from which visitors could easily travel to other wine-producing areas such as Napa Valley wine country. Santa Rosa is about three quarters of an hour's drive from the Pacific Ocean through Highway 12 by Sebastopol.

I left Santa Rosa in October 2002. After almost four years at Creekside, I felt it was time to move on. My time at Creekside was humbling. I left a new man. I was reborn, so to speak. I was transformed. My perspective on life was changed. My troubles paled in comparison to what I saw and experienced at the center. I have come across the phrase "under severe disorientation" in books and magazines. Creekside in Santa Rosa, California, was the place I saw it firsthand. Imagine what it would look like when someone pees and defecates on himself. The person is agitated and unaware of his surroundings, the resident is psychotic, he has lost touch with reality. People and objects around him are mere images he is not able to relate to. He is "dead" to the world, yet he is alive.

Someone close to you is mumbling incoherently to herself. When she stops mumbling, she starts to cry. Another resident is yelling at the top of his voice due to heightened psychosis or hallucination. There is that possibility a resident will sneak up on you and unleash an unsettling punch on your back. That is his own way of letting out steam. Yet amidst it all, you have to stay calm, keep your poise, and do the best you can to help.

One afternoon, residents were getting back into the unit from an outdoor break. I was standing in front of nurses' station A. Like a bolt out of the blue, for no reason at all, a short and stocky female resident walked up to where I was standing, got in my face, and, for about two minutes, spewed diatribes at me. I kept my cool. I did not take her action as personal. I was less than a year old at Creekside then. I attributed her behavior to the side effects of the medications she was taking. In situations like that, one developed a thick skin to handle challenges. It was part of the job.

The next day, the same woman sat by me in the dining room, telling me how her boyfriend made her laugh with the funny stories he told to her. If it was hatred she had in mind when she attacked me the previous day, I don't think she would have sat by me and told me about her hilarious boyfriend.

Since leaving Santa Rosa, I no longer take anything for granted. Life and time, I see as very precious. Good health and freedom are unquantifiable. Everyday activities such as taking a shower, making my own decisions, or going places without restrictions, I find invaluable. There were a few residents at Creekside who went out on pass and did not return. Some were found and brought back to Creekside. They all had one thing in common. They were all yearning for freedom. The ability to move to wherever they wanted without restriction, to make their own decisions, and do their own thing. They would have been able to lead normal lives if they were not mentally unstable. As a result of their mental incapacity, they were confined to an institution and could not lead normal lives, something a lot of people take for granted.

Anna once asked me to pray for her. I pray often now. I pray for the well-being of my loved ones. I try each day to do something positive to help my fellow man. I was once told to be close to my God through prayers and good deeds and that by so doing, there will be fewer emergencies in my own life. I subscribe to that philosophy.

CREEKSIDE

MENTAL HEALTH REHABILITATION PROGRAM

Oct. 10, 2002

To Whom It May Concern,

John Keshi has worked at Creekside Mental Health from 1/18/99 through 10/25/02 in the capacity of a Certified Nursing Assistant. His duties included supervising and teaching clients with a psychiatric diagnosis in their daily activities. John has been a very reliable employee and has no disciplinary action. He has chosen to seek other employement and will be missed at Creekside. His salary at this time is $12.50/ hr.

Sincerely Yours,

Assistant Director of Nursing

ROP
NORTH
ORANGE COUNTY
JOHN KESHI
STUDENT, VOCATIONAL NURSING

JOHN KESHI, MHW/CNA

Creekside Mental Health
Rehabilitation Program

ABOUT THE AUTHOR

John Keshi was born in Nigeria. He is an American citizen. He schooled at the University of Central Oklahoma in Edmond. This book was written while he was a resident in California. He now lives in New York.

9 781639 858965